PARIS
KNOPF CITYMAP GUIDES

W9-AUE-226

HOW TO USE THIS GUIDE

The **Welcome to Paris!** fold-out provides valuable information, handy tips and useful addresses to help you make the most of your visit.

The area sections **A, B, C, D, E, F, G** and **H** have a double-page of addresses (restaurants - listed in ascending order of price - cafés, bars, music venues and stores) as well as a fold-out map for the relevant area with the essential places to see (indicated on the map by a star ★). These places are by no means all that Paris has to offer but to us they are unmissable.

The grid-referencing system (**A** B2) makes it easy for the reader to pinpoint addresses quickly on the map.

The **Transport and hotels in Paris** fold-out provides all the practical information you need to find your way around the city and a selection of the best hotels.

The **Thematic index** lists all the sites and addresses featured in this guide.

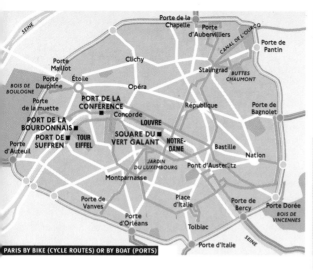

Map labels:

SEINE · Porte de la Chapelle · Porte d'Aubervilliers · Porte de Pantin · CANAL DE L'OURCQ · Clichy · Stalingrad · BUTTES CHAUMONT · Porte Maillot · Étoile · Opéra · Porte Dauphine · BOIS DE BOULOGNE · PORT DE LA CONFÉRENCE · République · Porte de Bagnolet · Porte de la muette · Concorde · LOUVRE · PORT DE LA BOURDONNAIS · PORT DE SUFFREN · TOUR EIFFEL · SQUARE DU VERT GALANT · NOTRE-DAME · Bastille · Porte d'Auteuil · JARDIN DU LUXEMBOURG · Nation · Pont d'Austerlitz · Montparnasse · Place d'Italie · Porte de Bercy · Porte Dorée · BOIS DE VINCENNES · Porte de Vanves · Porte d'Orléans · Tolbiac · SEINE · Porte d'Italie

PARIS BY BIKE (CYCLE ROUTES) OR BY BOAT (PORTS)

CHIC PARIS

Ave. Montaigne, Rue François-Ier (D C2)
The most famous names in *haute couture*.
Opéra, Madeleine (B C2)
Luxury foodstores, department stores.
Saint-Honoré (B C2)
The newest and best designers.
Pl. des Victoires (B E2)
Ready-to-wear, top labels.
Pl. Vendôme (B E2)
Hôtel Ritz, the big names in jewelry design.
Sèvres-Babylone (A A2)
Ready-to-wear, top designers and interior design.

TRENDY PARIS

Oberkampf (F B1)
The latest 'in' area.
Ménilmontant (G D6)
Attracts a new generation of party animals.
Bercy, Tolbiac (H E3)
Nightlife on the waterfront.
Le Marais (C E3)
Jewish and gay district.
Bastille (F B3)
Classic Paris nightlife.
Butte-aux-Cailles (H A4)
For the village atmosphere of yesteryear.

IMMORTAL PARIS

Latin Quarter (A C1)
Galleries, bookstores, literary cafés.
Champs-Élysées (D C1)
The famous triumphal arch.
Montparnasse (A A3)
The haunt of artists and bohemians for decades.

PARIS BY BOAT

'Bateaux-mouches'
Discover the city with a 1-hour cruise. Various companies (see map):
Vedettes de Paris
→ *Port de Suffren (7th)*
Tel. 01 44 18 08 03
M° Bir-Hakeim. Price: 50F
Bateaux-Parisiens
→ *Port de la Bourdonnais (7th)* Tel. 01 44 11 33 44
M° Trocadéro. Price: 50F
Vedettes du Pont-Neuf
→ *1, sq. du Vert-Galant (1st)*
Tel. 01 46 33 98 38
M° Pont-Neuf. Price: 50F
Compagnie des bateaux-mouches
→ *Port de la Conférence (7th)*
Tel. 01 42 25 96 10
M° Alma-Marceau. Price: 40F
Batobus
From the Eiffel Tower to the Hôtel-de-Ville in 6 stages.
→ *Port de la Bourdonnais (7th)* Tel. 01 44 11 33 99
M° Trocadéro. Per stage: 20F
Whole day: 60F

PARIS ON SKATES

It is still not clear where you are permitted to skate in Paris. Experienced skaters take advantage of side-walks, roads and cycle tracks alike.
Pari Roller (C C2)
→ Tel. 01 43 36 89 81
This company organizes a free 15-mile outing every Friday (departs 10pm from 40, ave. d'Italie). Not for beginners.
Nomades (C C2)
→ *37, bd Bourdon (4th)*
Tel. 01 44 54 07 44
Rental, classes and courses. Free outing on Sun (departs 2.30pm from in front of the store).

SHOPPING

Opening times
Mon–Sat 10am–7pm
Some stores close on Mon.
Late-night opening
On Thu. in most

department stores
(Le Printemps and
La Samaritaine are open
until 10pm and Les Galeries
Lafayette until 9pm).
Sales
Twice a year: January and July/Aug.
Department stores
BHV (**C** D3)
→ *52, rue de Rivoli (4th)*
La Samaritaine (**B** F4)
→ *19, rue de la Monnaie (1st)*
Le Bon Marché (**A** A2)
→ *22, rue de Sèvres (7th)*
Les Galeries Lafayette (**E** A6)
→ *40, bd Haussmann (9th)*
Le Printemps (**E** A6)
→ *64, bd Haussmann (9th)*

MARKETS

Flea markets (les 'puces')
Puces de Saint-Ouen
→ M° Porte-de-Saint-Ouen
Sat–Mon 7.30am–7pm.
The oldest and biggest of the city's flea markets. Quality goods spread over a dozen markets.

BY BOAT

BY BIKE

ETHNIC PARIS

**Avenue d'Ivry /
Porte de Choisy**
Little Chinatown.
**Rue and Bd de
Belleville**
Asia: on Rue de
Belleville. North Africa
on Bd de Belleville.
Rue des Rosiers
Jewish restaurants and
patisseries.
Passage Brady
India in miniature along
this attractive covered
passageway.
Barbès
Africa and North Africa
at Château-Rouge
market: various stores
and small restaurants.

PARIS IN FIGURES

- 33½ sq miles
- 20 arrondissements
- 80 quartiers (districts)
- 2 million inhabitants
in the city center
- 21 million visitors each
year ■ the 5th largest
city in the EU ■ 8 miles
of the Seine river

SEINE

XVIIe   XVIIIe   XIXe

VIIIe   IXe   X^e

BOIS DE
BOULOGNE   XVIe   Ier   IIe   IIIe   XXe

VIIe   IVe   XIe

VIe   V^e   XIIe

XVe   BOIS DE
VINCENNES

XIVe   XIIIe

SEINE

THE 20 ARRONDISSEMENTS

VIEWS OF THE CITY

Eiffel Tower (D B4)
The best view of Paris.
On a clear day you can
see for 40 miles.
Samaritaine (B F4)
From the circular terrace
on the 11th floor of this
department store.
Sacré-Cœur (E C3)
From the top of the dome.
Montparnasse (A A3)
From the top of the tower.
**Institut du Monde Arabe
(H** B1) Stunning view of
the Île Saint-Louis and Île
de la Cité from the 9th-
floor terrace.
Parc de Belleville (G D6)
Great views from the park
and Rue des Envierges.

GREEN SPACES

Parks and woods
Paris has around
5,440 acres of park and
woodland covering 20%
of the city's total area.

These include two huge
woodland areas: the Bois
de Boulogne and the Bois
de Vincennes and over
400 parks and gardens.
Opening times
Mon–Fri 7.30am–9.30pm,
Sat–Sun 9am–9.30pm
(until 5.30pm in winter).
Bois de Boulogne
→ Porte Dauphine / Porte
d'Auteuil. M° Porte-Maillot
2,088 acres of woodland
containing 9 miles of cycle
tracks, 17 miles of bridlepaths and numerous
footpaths. Bicycle rental
is available at the
entrance to the Jardin
d'Acclimatation and
at the lower lake's pier.
Bois de Vincennes
→ M° Porte-Dorée /
Château-de-Vincennes
2,500 acres of woodland,
pedestrian pathways,
bridlepaths and cycle
circuits. Lakes (boating),
playgrounds and a bird-
watching observatory

(near the Dauphine round-
about).

GUIDED TOURS

**Caisse Nationale des
Monuments Historiques
(C** F4)
→ Hôtel de Sully (4th)
Tel. 01 44 61 20 00
Organized tours of places
normally closed to the
public.
History of Paris
→ 82, rue Taitbout (9th)
Tel. 01 45 26 26 77
Guided theme-tours.
Program changes every
2 months.
Paris-Story
→ 11 bis, rue Scribe (9th)
Tel. 01 42 66 62 06
Apr–Oct 9am–8pm;
Nov–Mar 9am-6pm.
40-min film depicting
2,000 years of the history
of Paris, projected onto
a panoramic screen
with a soundtrack in
13 languages.

PARIS BY BICYCLE

Paris has around 90 miles
of cycle routes (see map
above). Some of the best:
• from Bd St-Germain to
Bastille (via the islands);
• from Bastille to La
Villette (via Bd Richard-
Lenoir, Canal St-Martin
and Canal de L'Ourcq);
• from Bastille to the
Promenade Plantée
(via Ave. Daumesnil
and Bd Diderot).
Rental, bike rides
**Paris à vélo,
c'est sympa (F** B3)
→ 37, bd Bourdon (4th)
Tel. 01 48 87 60 01
M° Bastille
Bicyle rental, guided tours
and organized bike rides
**Maison Roue Libre/RATP
(C** C2)
→ 95 bis, rue Rambuteau
(1st) Tel. 01 53 46 43 77
M° Châtelet-Les-Halles
Bicycle rental.

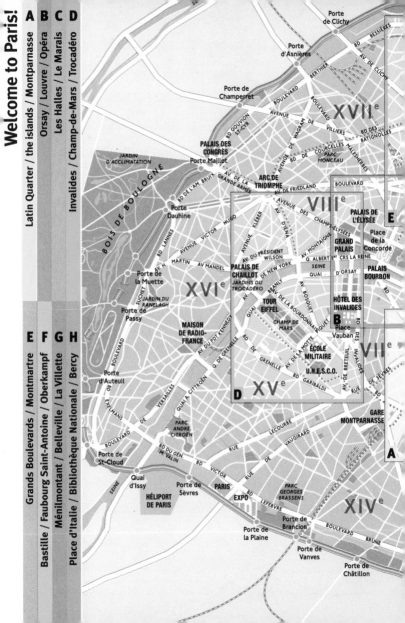

Welcome to Paris!

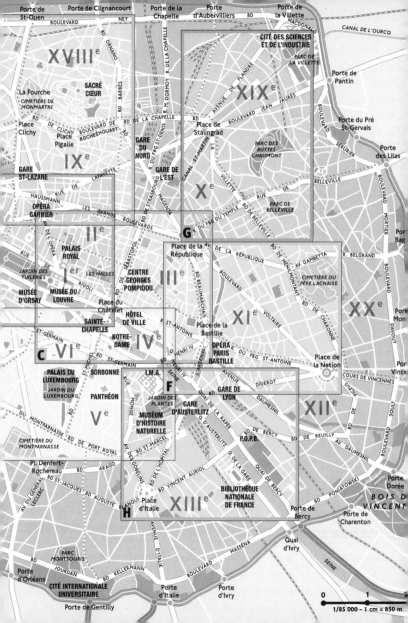

THE TOP OF LA SAMARITAINE

allows you free entry to
to museums/monuments
in and around Paris.

CALENDAR OF EVENTS

End February/March
Banlieue Bleues (jazz
festival at Seine Saint-
Denis); Agricultural Show.
Mid-March
International
contemporary art fair.
Early April
Paris Marathon.
End April/May
Paris fair.
End May/June
French Open Champion-
ship (tennis) at Rolland-
Garros.
June
Festival of Music (21st);
Cinema festival (last week-
end); Gay Pride (end June)
July
Jazz festival (La Villette);
Bastille Day (Firemen's
Ball and firework display,
13th, military parade,

14th); the Tour de France
arrives at the Champs-
Élysées end of July.
July/August
Film festival (La Villette);
Paris quartiers' summer
festival (dance, concerts).
September
Garden Show; Heritage
Open Days (properties
usually closed to the
public open for the day).
Mid-Sep./end-Dec.
Fall festival (dance,
theater, music).
October
Grape picking in
Montmartre (1st weekend).

USEFUL NUMBERS

Tourist office (**D C1**)
→ 127, ave. Champs-Élysées
(8th) Tel. 08 36 68 31 12
Lost property
→ Tel. 01 55 76 20 20
Police
→ Tel. 17
Samu (ambulance)
→ Tel. 15

WWW.

Sites on Paris
→ paris-web.com
→ paris-touristoffice.com
→ paris-france.org
**Cultural news, listings,
and information**
→ pariscope.com
→ fluctuat.net
→ cyberparis.com
→ cinetv.com
→ legrandrex.com
Museums
→ paris.org/Musees/
→ louvre.fr
→ musee-orsay.fr
→ cnac-gp.fr/Pompidou
Accommodation
→ france-hotel-guide.com
/75paccue.htm
→ homerental.fr
Going out
Parisian bistros
→ zingueurs.com
Trendy Paris
→ novaplanet.com
Cybercafés
→ cybercaptive.com

24-HOUR PARIS

Bakeries
Boulangerie de
l'Ancienne Comédie
→ 10, rue de l'Ancienne-
Comédie (6th)
Tel. 01 43 26 89 72. Daily.
Chemists
Pharmacie Rico
→ 6, pl. Félix Éboué (12th)
Tel. 01 43 43 19 03. Daily.
Pharmacie Derhy
→ 84, ave. des Champs-
Élysées (8th)
Tel. 01 45 62 02 41. Daily.
Restaurants
Au pied de cochon
→ 6, rue Coquillière (1st)
Tel. 01 40 13 77 00. Daily.
À la tour de Montlhéry
→ 5, rue des Prouvaires
Tel. 01 42 36 21 82 (1st)
Mon–Fri.
Tobacconists
La Favorite
→ 3, bd St-Michel (5th)
Tel. 01 43 54 08 02
Daily 7am–2am.
La Havane
→ 4, pl. de Clichy (9th)
Tel. 01 48 74 67 56
Mon–Thu 6.30am–5am,
Fri–Sun open 24 hours.

SUNDAY OPENING

Shopping
Some stores open along
the Champs-Élysées
(e.g. Virgin Méga Store),
on the Place des Vosges
and the Rue des Francs-
Bourgeois.
Museums
All museums open
on Sun.
Flea markets
Sat–Mon.
Skating or cycling
On Sun the banks of
the Seine are closed to
traffic.
→ Mar–Nov 10am–4pm.

MONMARTRE

BERCY VILLAGE

LE LOUVRE

Les Puces de Montreuil
→ M° Porte-de-Montreuil
Sat–Mon 8am–6pm.
The most popular of the
three flea markets: second-
hand clothes and mountains
of bric-à-brac.
Les Puces de Vanves
→ ave. Georges-Lafenestre
M° Porte-de-Vanves
Sat–Sun 7am–7pm.
Delightful bric-à-brac and
average antiques at
reasonable prices. Go to
Rue Marc-Saignier for
second-hand clothes and
discounted kitchen utensils.

Food markets
Each quartier has its own
market (daily or 2/3 times
a week).
→ rue Montorgueil (2nd)
Daily.
→ rue Mouffetard (5th)
Tue, Thu, Sat.
→ bd Richard-Lenoir (11th)
Thu, Sun.
→ rue d'Aligre (11th)
Tue–Sun.

→ bd de Belleville (20th)
Tue, Fri.
Flower markets
→ Île de la Cité
pl. Louis-Lépine (1st)
Mon–Sat 8am–7pm.
→ pl. de la Madeleine (8th)
Mon–Sat 8am–7.30pm.
→ pl. des Ternes (17th)
Tue–Sun 8am–7pm.

SHOWS

Reservations
FNAC(**A** A3)
→ 136, rue de Rennes (6th)
Tel. 08 36 68 04 56
Daily 24 hours.
Virgin Méga Store (**D** C1)
→ 52, ave. Champs-Élysées
(8th) Tel. 01 49 53 50 00
Daily noon–midnight.
Reductions
FNAC
→ Tel. 08 03 02 00 40
Standby seats available
3 hours before
performances. Up to
40% reduction on same-
or following-day tickets.

Theater kiosk
→ pl. de la Madeleine (8e) and
in front of Gare Montparnasse
(14th) Tue–Sat 12.30–8pm,
Sun 12.30–4pm.
50% reduction for same-
day performances.
National theaters
Limited number of seats at
50F, every Thu (from the
individual theaters).
Independent theaters
Seats at 70F for under
26-year-olds.
**Concert, movie, theater
information**
Officiel des spectacles
→ At newspaper kiosks,
every Wed, 2F
Listings of shows, plays,
concerts and movies...
Pariscope
→ At newspaper kiosks,
every Wed, 3F
Complete listings of cultural
events throughout Paris.
Lylo
→ FNAC, and bars
Every 3 weeks (free)
Lists all the city's concerts.

MUSEUMS

Opening times
Usually 10am–6pm. Closed
Mon (municipal museums)
or Tue (national museums).
Children
Most museums offer
guided tours, activities and
workshops for children.
Enquire at the individual
museums.
Concessions
Generally available to
students, 18–25 year-olds,
the over-60s and the
unemployed. Varies
depending on the museum.
Musée du Louvre (**B** E3)
→ Reduced-priced entry after
3pm every day, free on Sun.
Free entry
National museums
→ 1st Sun. of the month
Carte Musée Monuments
→ Pass available from
participating museums, FNAC,
tourist offices and subway
stations. Pass for 1, 3 or 5
days (80F, 160F or 240F).

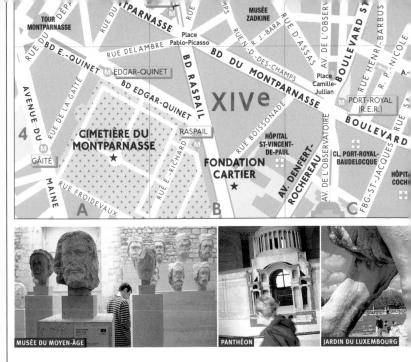

MUSÉE DU MOYEN-ÂGE

PANTHÉON

JARDIN DU LUXEMBOURG

★ Sainte-Chapelle (A D1)
→ 1, quai de l'Horloge (1ˢᵗ)
Tel. 01 53 73 78 50
Daily 10am–5pm.
This Gothic architectural
gem was built at the
request of Saint Louis
(1245–8) to house Christ's
Crown of Thorns. The use
of abutments instead of
flying buttresses, metal
frames and iron clamps
enabled the construction
of the extraordinary
50 ft-high stained-glass
windows. They depict
some 1,134 scenes
from the Old and New
testaments along with the
story of Louis IX receiving
the holy relics.

★ Pont-Neuf / Place Dauphine (A C1)
The oldest, longest and
most famous of Paris'
bridges was built in 1607
to allow King Henry IV to
cross from one bank to the
other. In 1985 Bulgarian
artist and sculptor Christo
completely wrapped the
bridge in fabric, turning it
into a work of art. At the far
end of the Île de la Cité is
Place Dauphine, the second
of the capital's royal squares,
built in 1607 in honor of the
Dauphin.

★ Cathédrale Notre-Dame (A E1)
→ 1, pl. du Parvis-de-Notre-
Dame (4ᵗʰ) Daily 8am–6.45pm.
This impressive cathedral,
begun in 1163, represents
Gothic architecture at its
most impressive. Here agin
the use of flying buttresses
permitted windows to be
introduced on a scale that
was previously unheard of.
The strikingly beautiful
rose window to the south,
the delicacy of the flying-
buttresses and the fragility
of the spire make this a
true masterpiece of Gothic
architecture.

★ Île Saint-Louis (A F1)
This tiny island was
nothing more than pasture-
land when Christophe
Marie began building a
village here in 1614. More
intimate than its neighbor
the Île de la Cité, it is full o
superb old houses, narrow
streets and flights of moss
steps leading down to the
Seine.

★ Église Saint-Germain des-Prés (A C1)
→ 3, pl. St-Germain-des-Pr
(6ᵗʰ) Tel. 01 43 25 41 71
Daily 8.30am–7.30pm.
The oldest church in Paris,
built in AD 990 on the
foundations of a
Merovingian basilica, it wa
uncovered in 1970. It has a
12th-century ambulatory
clocktower and choir, ribb
vaulting in the 17th-centur
nave and an 18th-century
presbytery.

SAINTE-CHAPELLE

PLACE DAUPHINE

Latin Quarter / the islands / Montparnasse

The Île de la Cité is the historic and geographic heart of Paris, filled with remnants of the old royal city. On the Rive Gauche (Left Bank) is St-Germain des-Prés with its post-war literary cafés, and the Quartier Latin with its art-house and experimental cinemas, universities and publishing houses. The Place de l'Odéon has held on to its former elegance, and the Rue St-André-des-Arts its medieval alleyways but the "Boul' Mich" (Bd St-Michel), joining onto the Luxembourg gardens, is now bereft of much of its former charm. It is worth making your way through the maze of streets around the Panthéon to the pretty Rue Mouffetard and its numerous little shops.

LA TAVERNE HENRY IV

KIOSQUE FLOTTANT

RESTAURANTS

Crêperie Josselin (**A** A3)
→ 67, rue du Montparnasse (14th)
Tel. 01 43 20 93 50
Tue-Fri noon–2.30pm,
6–11.30pm;
Sat-Sun noon–11pm.
No one should visit Montparnasse without stopping off to sample the famous galettes bretonnes (thick pancakes). Friendly atmosphere, typical Breton décor and superb crêpes. From 22F–57F per galette.

Taverne Henry IV (**A** D1)
→ 13, pl. du Pont-Neuf (1st) Tel. 01 43 54 27 90
Mon-Fri noon–8.30pm;
Sat noon–4pm. Closed Aug.
Robert Cointepas has manned the bar here for the past 40 years. More than 20 different types of wine available by the glass and delicious pork dishes from 30F.

Le Réminet (**A** E2)
→ 3, rue des Grands-Degrés (5th) Tel. 01 44 07 04 24
Closed Mon and Tue.
Chef Hugues Gourmay boldly marries different spices and flavors. Seasonal produce is cleverly integrated, with outstandingly delicious results. Reservations recommended in the evening. Set menu 110F, à la carte 210F.

Kiosque Flottant (**A** E2)
→ Port de Montebello (5th) Tel. 01 53 61 23 29
April–Sep: daily 10am–2pm
Sample a duck magret with raspberries in this splendid setting: a boat moored right at the foot of Notre-Dame.
À la carte 150F.

La Coupole (**A** C4)
→ 102, bd du Montparnasse (14th)
Tel. 01 43 20 14 20
Daily, continual service.
Once the meeting place of poets and writers in the 30s, today it still looks just the same, even after renovation. Art-Deco furnishings: painted pillars and chandeliers. Average cooking but good for people-watching.
Set menu 189F, 138F after 10.30pm.

Bouillon Racine (**A** D2)
→ 3, rue Racine (6th)
Tel. 01 44 32 15 60
Daily 7.30am–midnight.
A credit to Belgium, this stunning sea-green Art-Nouveau setting offers thirty different beers. Fish waterzooi (soup), knuckle of lamb confit and exquisite coffee liégeois (coffee ice cream with whipped cream) served

CAFÉ DE LA MAIRIE   MARCHÉ AUX FLEURS   BOUQUINISTES

by the jug. La Gueuze et
l'Écaille bar, adjacent to
the restaurant, has sea-
food dishes and sells an
impressive range of
Belgian beers. Set menu
189F.

CAFÉS, TEAROOMS

Le Flore (A B1)
→ 172, bd St-Germain (6th)
Tel. 01 45 48 55 26
Daily 7am–1.30am.
Once the haunt of Left-
Bank heroes such as
Picasso, Hemingway,
Camus and Sartre, this
café still attracts the city's
artists, intellectuals, and
writers who've just been
to see their editor in a
nearby publishing house.
The first floor tends to be
a quieter place to sit.
Pricey.
Café de la Mairie (A B2)
→ 8, pl. St-Sulpice (5th)
Tel. 01 43 26 67 82
Mon-Sat 7am–2pm.
Opposite the church of
St-Sulpice, this popular
café has become the
hang-out for literature
lovers. The ashes of Nina
Berberova were scattered
just in front under the
plane tree. Readings on
Tue evenings except in
summer. Pleasant terrace.
Charlotte de l'Île (A F2)
→ 24, rue Saint-Louis-en-

l'Île (4th) Tel. 01 43 54 25 83
Thu–Sun noon–8pm.
Tiny store with an
enchanting décor where
you can sample 36
blends of tea, divine hot
chocolate and delicious
fresh pastries.
La Viennoiserie (A C2)
→ 8, rue de l'École-de-
Médecine (6th)
Tel. 01 43 26 60 48
Mon-Fri 9am–7pm.
Tiny patisserie-cum-tea
room where a mixed
crowd of regulars and
students come on a daily
basis for the delicious
Jewish cakes, pastries, the
enormous ice-cream floats
and Viennese chocolates.
Savory tarts and salads at
lunchtime. Set menu 36F.

BARS, CINEMAS,
MUSIC VENUES

La Villa (A C1)
→ 29, rue Jacob (6th)
Tel. 01 43 26 60 00
Mon-Sat 6pm–2am.
In the magnificent vaulted
cellar of the modern hotel
Villa St-Germain this has
become since its opening
in 1991 one of the city's
leading jazz clubs.
Top-quality music and
performers.
**Caveau de
la Huchette** (A D1)
→ 5, rue de la Huchette

(5th) Tel. 01 43 26 65 05
Daily from 9pm.
This medieval cellar-club
has attracted rock 'n' roll
fans for generations. Jazz
and honky tonk piano at
weekends.
Polly Magoo (A D2)
→ 11, rue Saint-Jacques
(5th) Tel. 01 40 29 02 18
Daily noon–6am.
Discreet little bar with
nicotine-stained posters,
enticing nightowls in for
a last drink.
Le Champo (A D2)
→ 51, rue des Écoles (5th)
Tel. 01 43 54 51 60
The most famous art-
house and independent
cinema in the area.
Le P'tit Journal (A C3)
→ 71, bd St-Michel (5th)
Tel. 01 43 26 28 59
Mon-Sat 9am–2pm.
Atmosphere of 1950s
St-Germain-des-Prés
in this top-quality jazz
venue with the sounds
of Bolling, Zanini, Luter
and Bailey.

SHOPPING

Berthillon (A F2)
→ 31, rue St-Louis-en-l'Île
(4th) Tel. 01 43 54 31 61
Wed-Sun 10am–8pm.
Closed July-Aug.
Raspberry, mirabelle
plum, honey, fig, nougat...
This world-famous

ice-cream parlor boasts
some 70 different flavors.
Marché aux Fleurs
(A D1)
→ pl. Louis-Lépine (4th)
Daily 8am–7pm.
Flower market on the Île
de la Cité: a tiny jungle
right next to the Seine.
Bird market on Sun.
Bouquinistes (A C1-E2)
→ Thu-Sun.
Since the 19th century
this leafy row of second-
hand book stalls has
stood on the banks of the
Seine: forgotten novels,
anthologies of erotica,
old maps and pre-war
newspapers.
Le Bon Marché (A A2)
→ 24, rue de Sèvres (7th)
Tel. 01 44 39 80 00
Mon-Fri 9.30am–7pm;
Thu 9.30am–9pm;
Sat 9.30am–8pm.
Has become the most
chic department store,
complete with beauty
treatment spa and high-
quality delicatessen.
Christian Tortu (A C2)
→ Carrefour de l'Odéon
(6th) Tel. 01 43 26 02 56
Mon-Sat 9am–8pm;
Sun 11am–7pm.
The shop window of this
'artist' (you wouldn't dare
call him a florist) gives you
some idea of what the
Garden of Eden must have
been like.

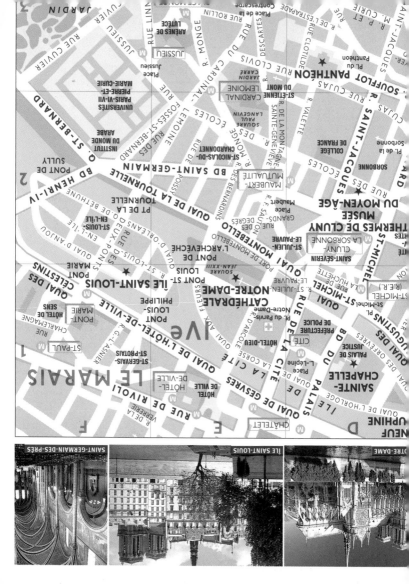

Place
Monge
PLACE MONGE
MUSÉUM NATIONAL
D'HISTOIRE NATURELLE
INSTITUT
MUSULMAN ET
MOSQUÉE
ÉCOLE NORMALE
SUPÉRIEURE
RUE ÉRASME
RUE CLAUDE-BERNARD
CENSIER-
DAUBENTON
ST-MÉDARD
RUE CENSIER
R. DAUBENTON
RUE BUFFON
RUE
GEOFFROY
POLIVEAU
HÔPITAL DU
VAL-DE-GRÂCE
UNIVERSITÉ
PARIS-III
RUE DU FER-À-MOULIN
CLINIQUE
ST-FRANÇOIS
SQUARE
SCIPION
BOULEVARD SAINT-MARCEL
ST-MARCEL
CLINIQUE
CHIRURGICALE
PÉAN
BD DE PORT-ROYAL
ORT-ROYAL
LES GOBELINS
XIIIe
0   150   300 m

FONDATION CARTIER

CIMETIÈRE DU MONTPARNASSE

Thermes de Cluny /
usée National du
oyen Âge (A D2)
6, pl. Paul-Painlevé (5th)
. 01 53 73 78 00
d-Mon 9.15am–5.45pm.
ght next to the remains of
e Gallo-Roman baths
nd–3rd century) stands
e Hôtel des Abbés de
uny (1485–1510), the
ost beautiful example of
edieval Parisian non-
igious architecture. Since
45 this has housed the
tional Museum of the
ddle Ages which contains
ries, heads of kings from
tre-Dame gold-work and
rics. The main attraction
he famous tapestry La

Dame à la Licorne (The Lady
and the Unicorn).
★ Panthéon (A D3)
→ pl. du Panthéon (5th)
Tel. 01 44 32 18 00
Daily 10am–6.15pm.
This church, built by Louis
XV, was not completed until
1789. Three years later the
Assembly dedicated it to
the memory of the great
names of the Revolution:
Mirabeau, Voltaire and
Rousseau. Its status as a
mausoleum was not made
official until 1885, in time to
accept the ashes of Victor
Hugo.
★ Jardin
du Luxembourg (A C3)
→ pl. Edmond-Rostand (6th)

Daily 8am–9.45pm (5.15pm
in winter).
The avenues of chestnut
trees, punctuated by an
astonishing series of
sculptures, and the English
garden and orchard with
710 varieties of apple trees
make this the city's most
romantic park. For over
100 years the central
ornamental lake, designed
by Le Nôtre (17th century),
has provided a favorite
sailing ground for model-
boat enthusiasts.
★ Fondation Cartier
(A B4)
→ 261, bd Raspail (14th)
Tel. 01 42 18 56 51
Daily noon–8pm.

This incredible construction
of glass and steel, designed
by Jean Nouvel in 1994,
houses more than 900
contemporary works of art
by 250 artists from all over
the world.
★ Cimetière du
Montparnasse (A A4)
→ 3, bd Edgar-Quinet (14th)
Tel. 01 44 10 86 50
Mon-Sun 9am–6pm
(5.30pm in winter).
A tribute to the writers and
artists who contributed to
this quartier's renown in the
19th and 20th centuries:
Baudelaire, Sartre, Beauvoir,
Maupassant, Dreyfus,
Brancusi and more recently,
Serge Gainsbourg.

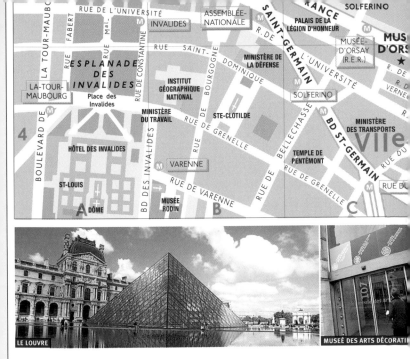

LE LOUVRE

MUSÉE DES ARTS DÉCORATI

★ **Église de la Madeleine** (**B** C2)
→ pl. de la Madeleine (8th)
Tel. 01 44 51 69 00
Mon-Sat 7.30am–1.30pm,
3.30–7pm.
Constant d'Ivry, commissioned by Napoleon I to build a monument to the glory of the French armies, came up with a design based on a Greek temple, similar to that of the National Assembly. Completed in 1842, the building, with neither clocktower nor cross on the exterior of the building, is now nevertheless used for religous worship.

★ **Place Vendôme** (**B** D2)
Superb and austere at the same time, this square, inaugurated in 1699 and built in the shape of a rectangle with its corners cut off, was originally a virtually enclosed space measuring 160 by 150 yds. Behind the uniform 80-ft high walls are hidden magnificent townhouses, one of which is the Hôtel Ritz at n° 15.

★ **Place de la Concorde** (**B** B3)
This busy major crossroads is, surprisingly, one of the most beautiful spots in Paris. It was designed for Louis XV in 1748. Contrary

to other royal squares it is only walled on one side in order to maintain the perspective of the triumphal axis: to the east are the Tuileries and the Louvre palace; to the west, the Champs-Élysées. The Luxor obelisk, presented by the viceroy of Egypt, was erected in the center of the square in 1836.

★ **Galerie du Jeu de Paume** (**B** C2)
→ pl. de la Concorde (1st)
Tel. 01 47 03 12 50
Tue noon–9.30pm;
Wed-Fri noon–7pm;
Sat-Sun 10am–7pm.
The Jeu de Paume, built under Napoleon III, has

been used for art exhibitions since the early 1900s. Magnificentl restored, it re-opened in 1991 and now mounts temporary exhibitions of contemporary art. Next door the Orangerie (close until 2002) houses Mone famous cycle of paintings Les Nymphéas.

★ **Jardins des Tuilerie** (**B** C3)
→ pl. du Carrousel (1st)
Daily 7.30am–9pm
(until 11.45pm July–Aug
and 7.30pm in winter).
In 1666, André Le Nôtre transformed the gardens the Château des Tuileries into a French-style garde

QUAI D'ORSAY

PONT DE LA
CONCORDE
INVALIDES (R.E.R.)

PONT
ALEXANDRE-III
PONT DES
INVALIDES

ORANGERIE

JARDINS
DES TUILERIES

COURS- -LA- -REINE

Pl. du
Canada

AV. DUTUIT

AV. W.-CHURCHILL

PLACE DE LA
CONCORDE

PETIT
PALAIS

UNIVERSITÉ
PARIS-IV

GALERIE
DU JEU
DE PAUME

CONCORDE

GRAND PALAIS

AV. DU GÉN. EISENHOWER

RUE DE

N.-D. DE
L'ASSOMPTION

RUE SAINT-HONORÉ

AVENUE DES CHAMPS-ÉLYSÉES

ROND-
POINT

RUE CAMBON

RUE DUPHOT

R. BOISSY-D'ANGLAS

RUE ROYALE

AVENUE GABRIEL

AV. F.-D.-ROOSEVELT

CHAMPS-ÉLYSÉES
CLEMENCEAU

TH. DU
ROND-

AVENUE

MADELEINE

BD DE LA MADELEINE

ÉGLISE DE
LA MADELEINE

Place de la
Madeleine

RUE DU FAUBOURG-ST-HONORÉ

AVENUE DE MARIGNY

AV. GABRIEL

R. DE PONTHIEU

RUE VIGNON

RUE TRONCHET

RUE DE SURÈNE

TR. DE LA
MADELEINE

PALAIS DE
L'ÉLYSÉE

AVENUE MATIGNON

RUE JEAN-MERMOZ

LA BOÉTIE

AV. F.-D.-ROOSEVELT

VIII

RUE DE L'ARCADE

R. PASQUIER

R. DE

RUE D'ANJOU

ARCHEVÊCHÉ
DE PARIS

Place
Beauvau

RUE DE PENTHIÈVRE

RUE DE MIROMESNIL

RUE DE PENTHIÈVRE

RUE DE LA BOÉTIE

RUE DE PONTHIEU

RUE DES MATHURINS

TEMPLE DU
ST-ESPRIT

R. CAMBACÉRÈS

ST-PHILIPPE-
DU-ROULE

RUE VIGNON

BD MALESHERBES

RUE D'ANJOU

CHAPELLE
EXPIATOIRE

LA BOÉTIE

RUE DE COURCELLES

RUE DE LA
PÉPINIÈRE

HAUSSMANN

BOULEVARD HAUSSMANN

RUE DE
ROME

RUE SA...

C   B   A

LA MADELEINE

PLACE VENDÔME

PLACE DE LA CONCORDE

B

Orsay / Louvre / Opéra

The proximity of the Louvre Museum has made this district a firm favorite with tourists, giving the souvenir stores the chance to invade the arcades along the Rue de Rivoli. Nevertheless, the area has lost none of its grandeur. La Madeleine boasts a number of designer tableware stores and luxurious delis; top stylists' outlets and fashion designers line Rue Saint-Honoré and the arcades of Place Vendôme shelter the Ritz Hotel and the most famous jewelry stores. To escape the uproar of the streets head for the peaceful gardens of the Palais-Royal or the Tuileries.

IL CORTILE   L'ENTRACTE

RESTAURANTS

Café Véry (B C3)
→ *Jardins des Tuileries (1ˢᵗ)*
Tel. 01 47 03 94 84
Daily noon–midnight.
A great place to enjoy the tranquility of the Tuileries gardens and sample a dish of chicken with morels or almond and cinnamon. Allow 70F for a full meal.

Il Cortile (B C2)
→ *37, rue Cambon (1ˢᵗ)*
Tel. 01 44 58 45 67
Mon-Fri noon–2.30pm, 7.30–10.30pm.
One of the best Italian restaurants in Paris, created by Alain Ducasse. Seasonal specialties: cuttlefish-ink cannelloni, risotto with asparagus, white Piedmont truffles... Lovely patio which is open in summer.
À la carte 300F.

Higuma (B E2)
→ *32 bis, rue St-Anne (1ˢᵗ)*
Tel. 01 47 03 38 59
Daily 11.30am–10pm.
Formica tables, cooks positioned in front of smoking woks ... *ramen* (flat noodles) and other Japanese specialties are served in this huge restaurant which attracts a clientele ranging from business people in a hurry to

young *manga*-magazine readers. Set menus 35F, 63F and 70F.

Le Rouge Vif (B C4)
→ *48, rue de Verneuil (7ᵗʰ)*
Tel. 01 42 86 81 87
Mon-Fri noon–2.15pm, 8–10.45pm; Sat 8–10.45pm.
Excellent food bought fresh from the markets, obliging service, a cozy place. Set lunch menu 95F, dinner 180F–220F.

Le Grand Véfour (B E2)
→ *17, rue de Beaujolais (1ˢᵗ)*
Tel. 01 42 96 56 27
Mon-Fri 12.30–2.15pm, 7.30–10.15pm.
One of the oldest and most beautiful restaurants in Paris, situated under the arcades of the Palais-Royal. Fabulous, listed interior decor; comfortable, plush banquettes. Guy Martin, from Savoy, creates simple dishes which make the most of the quality of his produce. Remarkable wine list. Reservation advised. Set lunch menu 350F. À la carte 700F.

TEAROOMS

Angelina (B C3)
→ *226, rue de Rivoli (1ˢᵗ)*
Tel. 01 42 60 82 00
Daily 9am–7pm.
Opened in 1903 under the arcades in Rue de Rivoli,

FLANN O' BRIEN'S COLETTE DIDIER LUDOT

this English tearoom serves some of the best hot chocolate in Paris (36F), along with excellent desserts. Chocolates and pastries to go.

CAFÉS, BARS, MUSIC VENUES

Café Marly (B E3)
→ *Palais du Louvre*
93, rue de Rivoli (1st)
Tel. 01 49 26 06 60
Daily 8am–2pm.
An exceptional setting to stop for a drink and view I.M. Pei's pyramid and the French sculpture rooms of the Louvre museum. Pleasant service. Coffee 19F, draught beer 32F, lunch menu 250F.

L'Entracte (B E3)
→ *47, rue de Montpensier (1st) Tel. 01 42 97 57 76*
Mon–Fri 10am–2am;
Sat–Sun noon–1am.
This café has been around for centuries. Actors and audience alike from the Comédie-Française and the Théâtre du Palais-Royal come here for pre- or post-show drinks. Fresh, homemade food. Coffee 12F, draught beer 18F after 7.30pm.

Flann O' Brien's (B F3)
→ *6, rue Bailleul (1st)*
Tel. 01 42 60 13 58
Daily 4pm–2am.

Excellent Irish pub serving the smoothest Guinness in town (a pint: 39F). Darts board upstairs and excellent live music most nights.

Opéra Garnier (B D1)
→ *Palais Garnier*
8, rue Scribe (8th)
Tel. 01 47 42 07 02
Impressive neo-Renaissance and Baroque building dating from 1858. The auditorium ceiling was repainted by Chagall in 1964. Ballet, dance and opera performances. The library, museum, Grand Staircase and Foyer are open to the public.

SHOPPING

Samaritaine (B F4)
→ *19, rue de la Monnaie (1st) Tel. 01 40 41 20 20*
Mon–Sat 9.30am–7pm (until 10pm Thu).
Department store situated right next to the Seine. You can buy anything you could possibly need here. Magnificent view of Paris from the roof-terrace.

Anna Joliet (B E2)
→ *9, rue de Beaujolais (1st)*
Tel. 01 49 27 98 60
Mon–Sat 10am–7pm.
Music boxes that will take you back to your childhood. Over 60 different

tunes can be heard escaping from this little store hidden away beneath the arcades of the Palais-Royal. Expect to pay around 200F.

Sennelier (B D4)
→ *3, quai Voltaire (7th)*
Tel. 01 42 60 72 15
Mon 2–7.30pm;
Tue–Sat 9.30am–2pm.
Walking into this three-story store is like opening an old paint box. Since 1887 Sennelier has supplied artists with papers, paints, pastels or lapis lazuli in powder form (at 2,000F for 10 gms) ... all with the Sennelier stamp.

Fauchon (B C2)
→ *24, pl. de la Madeleine (8th) Tel. 01 47 42 60 11*
Mon–Sat 9.30am–7pm (tearoom 8am–7pm).
The most famous delicatessen in Paris: preserves, pastries, cold meats, wine, tea. An incredible range of fine and expensive goods.

Shiseido (B E3)
→ *142, galerie de Valois (1st) Tel. 01 49 27 09 09*
Mon–Sat 10am–7pm.
Under the arcades of the Palais-Royal, a treasure trove of exotic perfumes created by Serge Lutens for Shiseido. Some scents on sale here are exclusive to this store.

Colette (B D3)
→ *213, rue Saint-Honoré (1st) Tel. 01 55 35 33 90*
Mon–Sat 10.30am–7.30pm.
If it is tomorrow's fashion in clothes, art, cosmetics, jewelry, etc... Colette will have it before anybody else, and sell it ... at a price. There is a mineral water bar – the most exclusive of course – a dining room in the basement and a designers' exhibition on the 1st floor. Worth a visit, just for fun.

Didier Ludot (B E3)
→ *24, galerie Montpensier (1st) Tel. 01 42 96 06 56*
Mon–Sat 10.30am–7pm.
Second-hand clothes, footwear, bags and cases whether by Chanel, Hermès, Balenciaga, Courrèges... Didier Ludot is a genuine collector of the best designs by the biggest names.

Le Louvre des Antiquaires (B E3)
→ *2, pl. du Palais-Royal (1st) Tel. 01 42 97 27 00*
Tue–Sun 11am–7pm.
Closed Aug.
Two hundred and fifty antiques dealers under the roof of a former department store. Spread over three floors are Louis XV furniture, china, gold, jewelry ...

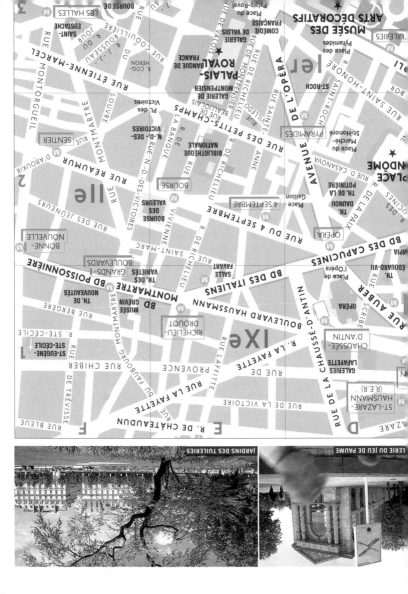

JARDINS DES TUILERIES

...ERIE DU JEU DE PAUME

MUSÉE DU LOUVRE
DU CARROUSEL
QUAI DES TUILERIES
PONT ROYAL
PONT DU CARROUSEL
PALAIS DU LOUVRE
LOUVRE
Pl. du Louvre
ST-GERMAIN-L'AUXERROIS
DE RIVOLI
RUE BAILLEUL
R. DU ROULE
RUE DU PONT-NEUF
CHÂTELET
DES HALLES
Q. DU LOUVRE
Q. VOLTAIRE
QUAI MALAQUAIS
RUE DE LILLE
RUE DE VERNEUIL
UNIVERSITÉ
Pl. de l'Institut
PONT DES ARTS
PONT-NEUF
RUE DE LA MONNAIE
Q. DE LA MÉGISSERIE
TH. DU CHÂTELET
PONT-NEUF
Pl. du Pont-Neuf
INSTITUT DE FRANCE
Q. DE CONTI
ÉCOLE DES BEAUX ARTS
RUE DES SAINTS-PÈRES
RUE BONAPARTE
R. DE SEINE
R. MAZARINE
HÔTEL DES MONNAIES
Q. DES GRANDS-AUGUSTINS
QUAI DE L'HORLOGE
ÎLE DE LA CITÉ
RUE JACOB
RUE DES
UNIVERSITÉ PARIS-V
0
150
300 m
D
E
F
4

RDINS DU PALAIS-ROYAL

MUSÉE D'ORSAY

d opened up the view to e west with a road which er became the Champs-ysées. The octagonal ce, the terraces running ong the Seine and the e de Rivoli, the merous chestnut and e trees growing on her side of the central enue all convey the mance of times past.

Musée du Louvre (**B** E3)
cour Napoléon (1st)
. 01 40 20 50 50
n & Wed 9am–9.30pm, u-Sun 9am–5.30pm.
e largest museum in e world. The Louvre's llections stretch from e ancient civilizations of the Mediterranean basin to the first half of the 19th century, today completed by a new section on primitive arts. Over 800 years of French history are contained within these walls. The Cour Carrée, first begun under François I, is one of the best examples of Renaissance architecture. In 1989 Ieoh Ming Pei came up with a daring design for the Napoleon courtyard, erecting a glass pyramid at its center.

★ **Musée des Arts Décoratifs** (**B** D3)
→ *Palais du Louvre 116, rue de Rivoli (1st)*
Tel. 01 44 55 57 50
Daily 11am–6pm.
Unique collection of furniture, painting and *objets d'art* dating from the Middle Ages to the present day. Entrance tickets also give access to the Fashion and Textile and Advertising museums.

★ **Palais-Royal** (**B** E3)
→ *pl. du Palais-Royal (2nd)*
The peaceful atmosphere of the gardens and the adjacent galleries is deceptive. It was under these arcades that Parisian commerce spread in 1780, as did gambling and prostitution, while in the clubs ideas of a revolution were beginning to circulate. Home of Cardinal Richelieu, then of the Orléans family, the palace now houses the Council of State and the Ministry of Culture, whose windows overlook the main courtyard, redesigned by Buren in 1986.

★**Musée d'Orsay** (**B** C4)
→ *1, rue de Bellechasse (7th)*
Tel. 01 40 49 48 14
Tue-Sun 10am–5.30pm (Thu 10am–9.45pm).
The conversion of this former railway station into a museum began in 1977. Opened in 1986, it has an unbeatable collection of art spanning the second half of the 19th century.

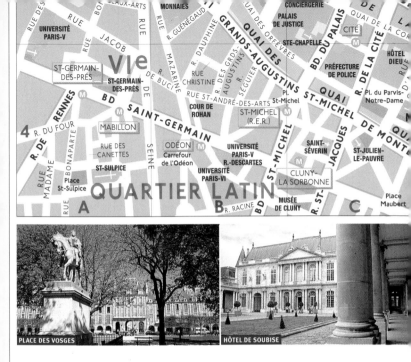

Map labels:
BEAUX-ARTS · MONNAIES · CONCIERGERIE · PALAIS DE JUSTICE · QUAI DE LA COR...
RUE DES... · RUE · BO... · R. GUÉNÉGAUD · QUAI DES ORFÈVRES · STE-CHAPELLE · QUAI DE LA CITÉ · CITÉ
UNIVERSITÉ PARIS-V · RUE · JACOB · RUE DAUPHINE · GRANDS-AUGUSTINS · BD. DU PALAIS · HÔTEL DIEU
VIe · RUE DE BUCIE · RUE MAZARINE · RUE CHRISTINE · RUE DES GRDS-AUGUSTINS · R. SÉGUIER · QUAI DES GRANDS-AUGUSTINS · PRÉFECTURE DE POLICE · DE LA CITÉ
ST-GERMAIN-DES-PRÉS · ST-GERMAIN-DES-PRÉS · RUE ST-ANDRÉ-DES-ARTS · Pl. St-Michel · QUAI ST-MICHEL · R. Pl. du Parvis-Notre-Dame
RENNES · BD · SAINT-GERMAIN · COUR DE ROHAN · ST-MICHEL (R.E.R.) · DE MONT...
R. DU FOUR · DE · BONAPARTE · MABILLON · SEINE · ODÉON · Carrefour de l'Odéon · UNIVERSITÉ PARIS-V R.-DESCARTES · BD ST-MICHEL · SAINT-SÉVERIN · ST-JULIEN-LE-PAUVRE · QUAI
RUE DES CANETTES · UNIVERSITÉ PARIS-VI · CLUNY-LA SORBONNE
RUE MADAME · ST-SULPICE · Place St-Sulpice · QUARTIER LATIN · R. RACINE · MUSÉE DE CLUNY · R. ST-JACQUES · Place Maubert
A · B · C

PLACE DES VOSGES

HÔTEL DE SOUBISE

★ Les Halles / Montorgueil (C C2)
→ Rue Berger (1st) /
R ue Montorgueil (1st)
With its busy market, the
Rue Montorgueil, recently
pedestrianized, is perhaps
the last vestige of the old
Halles. Always lively.

★ Centre Georges-Pompidou (C D3)
→ Rue Saint-Martin (4th)
Tel. 01 44 78 12 33
Mon, Wed-Sun. 11am–9pm
(museum); noon–10pm (Bpi)
Opened in 1977 this very
controversial avant-garde
building was a joint
venture between architects
Renzo Piano and Richard
Rogers, in response to
Pompidou's (the then
president's) wish to
establish a multi-discipline
cultural center in Paris
which would be both a
museum and an art center.
The Musée National d'Art
Moderne and the Center
de Création Industrielle are
both based here along with
a public information library,
movie theater and regular
children's workshops.
The layout was entirely
reorganized in 1999 by
Renzo Piano and Jean-
François Beaudin.
Panoramic views of Paris
from the restaurant.

★ Hôtel-de-Ville (C D3)
→ Pl. de l'Hôtel-de-Ville (4th)
Until 1778 the Place de
l'Hôtel-de-Ville was named
Place de Grève (shore)
because of its location on
the river banks of the
Seine. In 1357 it became
the seat of municipal
power. The site later
became a platform for riots
and demonstrations
('grève' also means 'strike')
and, until 1830, public
executions. The interior of
the building, refurbished in
the late 19th-century,
contains an abundance of
gilt, wood-paneling and
Baccarat chandeliers, the
spoils of the 3rd Republic.
Each winter the area in
front of the town hall is
turned into a free public
skating rink.

★ Hôtel de Sens (C E4)
→ 1, rue du Figuier (4th)
Tel. 01 42 78 14 60
Closed Sun.
This 15th-century buildin...
still has corbeled turrets,
a Gothic porch and
a cobbled courtyard
where Queen Margot on...
unhitched her carriage.
Today it houses the Forn...
Library of Decorative Arts

★ Hôtel de Sully (C F...
→ 62, rue St-Antoine (4th)
Tel. 01 44 61 20 00. Daily.
Dating from the 17th-
century this is one of the
most beautiful and
impressive townhouses

c

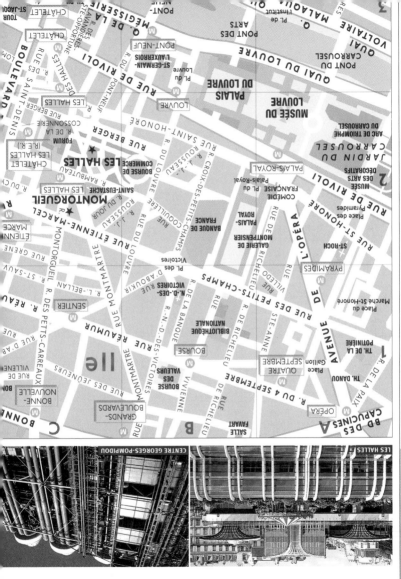

CENTRE GEORGES-POMPIDOU

LES HALLES

The area around the Halles has been the focus of major building projects since the 1960s and makes up the heart of modern Paris. The Baltard houses, the churches of St-Eustache and of Beaubourg (the village) have all gone. The largest pedestrianized area in Europe stretches between Rue Montorgueil and the gates of St-Martin and St-Denis. Pop into the Georges-Pompidou center or explore the old quartier of Le Marais, a listed area since 1962. Here the 17th-century townhouses and narrow winding streets contain a mixture of Jewish stores, quirky, trendy boutiques, antique dealers and gay bars.

TRUMILOU   L'ESCARGOT DE MONTORGUEIL

RESTAURANTS

Minh Chau (C D3)
→ 10, rue de la Verrerie (4th) Tel. 01 42 71 13 30
Daily 9am–midnight.
Tiny Vietnamese restaurant where you can drop in for a quick bite to eat: peppered pork or shrimp curry (20–25F) accompanied by a cup of tea (3F). Very friendly.

Chez Marianne (C E3)
→ 2, rue des Hospitalières-Saint-Gervais (4th)
Tel. 01 42 72 18 86 Daily.
Charming delicatessen where you can sample Jewish and Eastern European fare. An abundance of *meze*: fallafel, *kefta*, tabouleh, stuffed vine leaves... You can also take out. Good choice for vegetarians. Book in advance. À la carte 55–75F.

Jo Goldenberg (C E3)
→ 7, rue des Rosiers (4th)
Tel. 01 48 87 20 16
Daily 9am–midnight.
A shrine to Ashkenazi cooking: borscht, stuffed carp, chopped liver and onions, chicken soup. Inviting atmosphere and music. Daily special 80F.

Trumilou (C B2)
→ 84, quai de l'Hôtel-de-Ville (4th) Tel. 01 42 77 63 98
Daily noon–3pm, 7–11pm.
Small dishes to suit all budgets. Traditional and simple cuisine, just like home-cooking. Set menus 80F, 98F.

Chez Omar (C E2)
→ 47, rue de Bretagne (3rd) Tel. 01 42 72 36 26
Closed Sun lunch.
Traditional brasserie and the best couscous in Paris, cooked by Omar himself. À la carte 120F.

La Mule du Pape (C F3)
→ 8, rue du Pas de la Mule (3rd) Tel. 01 42 74 55 80
Mon-Fri 11am–6pm, 7–11pm
Sat 11am–11pm;
Sun 11am–7pm.
A few yards away from the Place des Vosges, this is a small, homely, cozy restaurant. Provençale specialties; home-made desserts. Salad with foie gras and one glass of wine 100F. À la carte 150F. Wines by the glass. It is advisable to book.

L'Escargot de Montorgueil (C C2)
→ 38, rue Montorgueil (1st) Tel. 01 42 36 83 51
Daily noon–3pm, 7–11pm.
An excellent place to taste delicious Burgundy snails in an 1870s setting.

TEAROOMS

L'Ébouillanté (C D3)
→ 6, rue des Barres (4th)

BOUILLANTÉ — **LE LATINA** — **VILLAGE SAINT-PAUL**

Tel. 01 42 71 09 69
Tue-Sun noon–10pm (9pm in winter).
In a pedestrianized street opposite the church of St-Gervais-St-Protais. Mellow jazz is played in the book-lined interior, decorated in blue. The terrace is perfect for afternoon tea. Set menu 75F.

Marais Plus (C E3)
→ *20, rue des Francs-Bourgeois (3rd)*
Tel. 01 48 87 01 40
Daily 10am–7.30pm.
Store and tearoom selling fascinating and unusual toys, large and small. Exquisite savory and sweet tarts (eat in or take out).

Le Loir dans la Théière (C E3)
→ *3, rue des Rosiers (6th)*
Tel. 01 42 72 90 61
Mon-Fri 11.30am–7pm;
Sat-Sun 10am–7pm.
Sink into the comfortable old leather armchairs and enjoy a salad or delicious pastry. Excellent service. Savory tarts 48F, salads 45F.

CAFÉS, BARS, THEATERS, MUSIC VENUES

Web Bar (C E2)
→ *32, rue de Picardie (3rd)*
Tel. 01 42 72 66 55

Daily 11.30am–2am.
A heaven for cyberfans, this old silversmith work shop, converted into an Internet café, has plenty more to offer: poetry nights, debates, chess, concerts, art exhibitions…

Café Beaubourg (C D3)
→ *43, rue St-Merri (4th)*
Tel. 01 48 87 63 96
Daily 8am–1am.
Opposite the Pompidou center, this is the most chic café in the area, with an extraordinary design by architect Christian de Portzamparc.
À la carte 175F.

Duc des Lombards (C C3)
→ *42, rue des Lombards (1st) Tel. 01 42 33 22 88*
Tue-Sat from 9pm;
Sun-Mon: times vary depending on the program.
The poster-covered walls trace the history of jazz. Innovative line-up with a bias toward modern European jazz. Entrance 100F; drinks 28F.

Le Petit Opportun (C C3)
→ *15, rue des Lavandières-Sainte-Opportune (1st)*
Tel. 01 42 36 01 36
Tue–Sat from 10.30pm.
Small club that welcomes musicians from the French jazz scene, both newcomers and old timers alike: swing,

bebop, New Orleans jazz. Entrance 50–80F.

Café de la Gare (C D3)
→ *41, rue du Temple (4th)*
Tel. 01 42 78 52 51
Daily 8pm and 10pm.
The nicest of the *café-théâtres*, this venue has hosted comics, popular theater and children's shows (at 3pm) for 30 years. Entrance 100F.

Le Latina (C D3)
→ *20, rue du Temple (4th)*
Tel. 01 42 78 47 86
Since 1913 Le Latina has screened the best of Italian, Spanish, Portuguese and Latin-American films. On the first floor is a bar and dance floor complete with strutting tango dancers.

Amnesia (C E3)
→ *42, rue Vieille-du-Temple (4th) Tel. 01 42 72 16 94*
Daily 9.30am–2am.
Ivy-fronted gay bar. A colorful clientele and 1980s music in the basement. Salad and daily specials 45F.

SHOPPING

Forum des Halles (C C2)
→ *Rues Berger and Rambuteau (1st) Mon–Sat.*
Several hundred stores (one of which is FNAC), movie theater and swimming pool.

Mariage Frères (C D3)
→ *30, rue du Bourg-Tibourg (4th) Tel. 01 42 72 28 11*
Daily 10.30am–7.30pm (store), noon–7pm (rest).
Magnificent colonial-style store packed with huge round pots containing 350 varieties of tea from all over the world. Sample in house or take out. Brunch on Sun from noon–6.30pm.
À la carte 80–150F.

BHV (C D3)
→ *52, rue de Rivoli (4th)*
Tel. 01 42 77 44 79
Mon–Sat 9.30am–7pm
The place for DIY enthusiasts. The Bazar de l'Hôtel-de-Ville, right in the heart of Paris, also sells high fashion, toys perfume, books and electric appliances.

Village Saint-Paul (C E4)
→ *Rues Charlemagne and Saint-Paul (4th) Thu-Mon.*
An entire colony of little antique stores situated between Rue Saint-Paul and Rue Charlemagne along quiet passageways and courtyards.

Finkelstajn (C E3)
→ *27, rue des Rosiers (4th)*
Tel. 01 42 72 78 91
Wed-Mon noon–7pm.
The best Jewish deli in Paris: Russian and central European specialties.

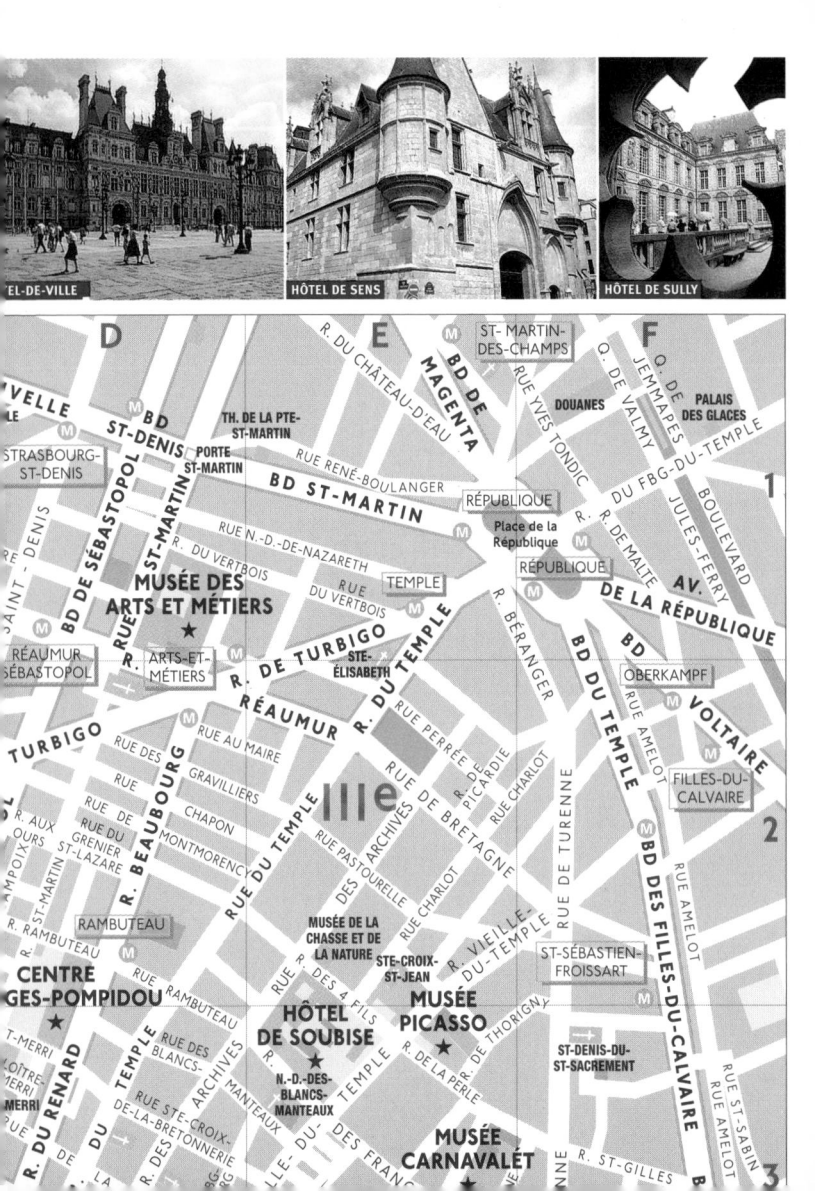

HÔTEL-DE-VILLE

HÔTEL DE SENS

HÔTEL DE SULLY

D

E

F

VELLE
LE

STRASBOURG-
ST-DENIS

BD ST-DENIS

TH. DE LA PTE-
ST-MARTIN

PORTE
ST-MARTIN

RUE RENÉ-BOULANGER

R. DU CHÂTEAU-D'EAU

BD DE MAGENTA

ST-MARTIN-
DES-CHAMPS

RUE YVES TONDIC

DOUANES

Q. DE JEMMAPES

Q. DE VALMY

PALAIS
DES GLACES

BD ST-MARTIN

DU FBG-DU-TEMPLE

BOULEVARD

RÉAUMUR
SÉBASTOPOL

BD DE SÉBASTOPOL

SAINT - DENIS

RUE - DENIS

BD ST-MARTIN

RUES ST-MARTIN

R. DU VERTBOIS

RUE N.-D.-DE-NAZARETH

RUE
DU VERTBOIS

RÉPUBLIQUE

Place de la
République

TEMPLE

JULES-FERRY

R. DE MALTE

RÉPUBLIQUE

AV. DE LA RÉPUBLIQUE

1

MUSÉE DES
ARTS ET MÉTIERS
★

ARTS-ET-
MÉTIERS

R. DE TURBIGO

STE-
ÉLISABETH

R. DU TEMPLE

R. BÉRANGER

RÉAUMUR

RUE PERRÉE

R. DE
PICARDIE

RUE CHARLOT

BD DU TEMPLE

OBERKAMPF

RUE AMELOT

BD VOLTAIRE

2

TURBIGO

RUE DES
GRAVILLIERS

RUE AU MAIRE

R. AUX
OURS
ST-MARTIN
AMPOIX

RUE DE
GRENIER
ST-LAZARE

R. DU
BEAUBOURG

CHAPON

MONTMORENCY

RUE DU TEMPLE

DES ARCHIVES

RUE PASTOURELLE

RUE DE BRETAGNE

R. DE
P.
PICARDIE

RUE CHARLOT

RUE DE TURENNE

BD DU TEMPLE

FILLES-DU-
CALVAIRE

RUE AMELOT

BD DES FILLES-DU-CALVAIRE

RAMBUTEAU

CENTRE
GES-POMPIDOU
★

RUE RAMBUTEAU

R. RAMBUTEAU

MUSÉE DE LA
CHASSE ET DE
LA NATURE

R. DES 4 FILS

STE-CROIX-
ST-JEAN

RUE CHARLOT

R. VIEILLE-
DU-TEMPLE

ST-SÉBASTIEN-
FROISSART

RUE ST-SABIN

RUE AMELOT

T-MERRI
LOÎTRE-
MERRI
MERRI

R. DU RENARD

TEMPLE
DU

RUE DES
BLANCS-

ARCHIVES

RUE STE-CROIX-
DE-LA-BRETONNERIE

MANTEAUX

HÔTEL
DE SOUBISE
★

N.-D.-DES-
BLANCS-
MANTEAUX

R. DE LA PERLE

TEMPLE-DU-

DES FRAN

MUSÉE
PICASSO
★

DE THORIGNY

ST-DENIS-DU-
ST-SACREMENT

3

R. ST-GILLES

MUSÉE
CARNAVALET
★

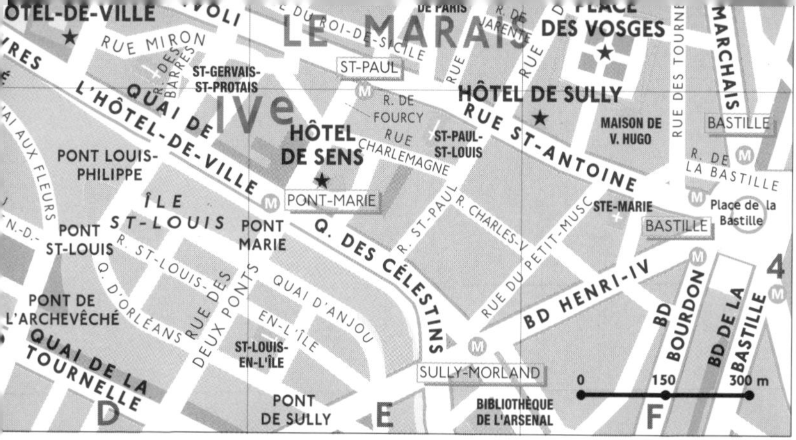
OTEL-DE-VILLE
VOLI
LE MARAIS
DE PARIS
PLACE DES VOSGES
RUE MIRON
R. DES BARRES
ST-GERVAIS-ST-PROTAIS
DU ROI-DE-SICILE
ST-PAUL
R. DE FOURCY
HÔTEL DE SULLY
RUE ST-ANTOINE
MAISON DE V. HUGO
BASTILLE
RUE DES TOURNE
MARCHAIS
QUAI DE L'HÔTEL-DE-VILLE
IVe
HÔTEL DE SENS
RUE CHARLEMAGNE
ST-PAUL-ST-LOUIS
PONT LOUIS-PHILIPPE
QUAI AUX FLEURS
ÎLE ST-LOUIS
PONT-MARIE
R. DE LA BASTILLE
Place de la Bastille
STE-MARIE
BASTILLE
PONT ST-LOUIS
PONT MARIE
Q. DES CÉLESTINS
R. ST-PAUL
R. CHARLES-V
RUE DU PETIT-MUSC
R. ST-LOUIS-EN-L'ÎLE
QUAI D'ANJOU
BD HENRI-IV
BD BOURDON
BD DE LA BASTILLE
4
PONT DE L'ARCHEVÊCHÉ
Q. D'ORLÉANS
RUE DES DEUX PONTS
ST-LOUIS-EN-L'ÎLE
QUAI DE LA TOURNELLE
SULLY-MORLAND
0
150
300 m
PONT DE SULLY
BIBLIOTHÈQUE DE L'ARSENAL
D
E
F

ISÉE CARNAVALET

MUSÉE PICASSO

MUSÉE DES ARTS ET MÉTIERS

e Marais and was a nter of society life in the ne of the dukes of Sully. e main courtyard, with Renaissance décor, the rden and the orangery e all still intact. Today it the home of the Caisse tionale des Monuments storiques (state-funded fice which protects the tural heritage).

Place des Vosges
F3)
ick façades, high French bles, arcaded galleries... e sumptuous former ce Royale has retained the splendor of the days Henry IV's reign. At n° 6, tor Hugo's house has been turned into a little museum.

★ **Hôtel de Soubise**
(**C** E3)
→ *60, rue des Francs-Bourgeois (3rd)*
Tel. 01 40 27 62 18
Mon, Wed-Fri 10am-5.45pm (from 1.45pm at weekends).
Built by Boffand in 1735, this is a Parisian *rocaille*-style masterpiece. The outside of the building, with its austere air, is in stark contrast to the extravant interior decor with its white and gold paneling and allegorical stucco *haut-reliefs* in the salon. The National Archives and the Museum of French History are now housed here.

★ **Musée Carnavalet**
(**C** E3)
→ *23, rue de Sévigné (3rd)*
Tel. 01 44 59 58 58
Tue-Sun 10am–5.40pm.
Rich collection of art centered around Parisian history, archeology, architecture, society and culture.

★ **Musée Picasso** (**C** E3)
→ *5, rue de Thorigny (3rd)*
Tel. 01 42 71 25 21
Wed-Mon 9.30am–5.30pm (until 8pm Thu).
Superb Marais townhouse entirely dedicated to Picasso. It contains a chronological review of the work of the artist from 1894 to 1972. The scope of the works makes this the most important collection of Picasso's work in the world.

★ **Musée des Arts et Métiers** (**C** D1)
→ *60, rue Réaumur (3rd)*
Tel. 01 53 01 82 00
Tue-Sun 10am–6pm (until 9.30pm Thu).
Discover Pascal's calculating machine, Lavoisier's laboratory, Foucault's pendulum and 84,000 other objects and documents following the great technological inventions from the 16th century to the present day.

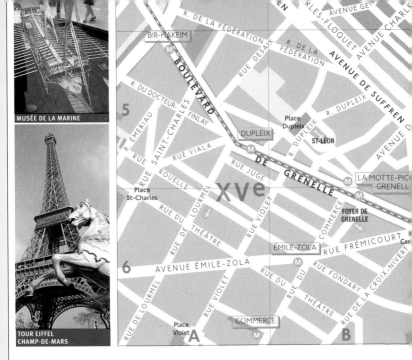

MUSÉE DE LA MARINE

TOUR EIFFEL
CHAMP-DE-MARS

★ **Arc de Triomphe** (**D** B1)
→ *Pl. du Général-de-Gaulle
(8th) Tel. 01 55 37 73 77
Summer: daily 9.30am–11pm
Winter: daily 10am–10.30pm.*
This huge neoclassical arch
dating from the Napoleonic
era dominates the Champs-
Élysées. Magnificent view
from the top. Under the
platform a museum traces
the building's history.
★ **Trocadéro** (**D** A3)
On a hilltop overlooking
the Seine the two wings of
the impressive Palais de
Chaillot encircle the
Trocadéro's esplanade. All
year round this is a favorite
spot for roller-skaters; in
summer, the ornamental

lakes and fountains
become improvized
swimming pools.
★ **Musée de la Marine**
(**D** A3)
→ *17, pl. du Trocadéro (16th)
Tel. 01 53 65 69 69
Wed-Mon 10am–5.50pm.*
First begun in the Louvre in
1937, it moved to the Palais
de Chaillot in 1997. This
museum is famous for its
fascinating collection of
model boats tracing the
history of seafaring and
for its beautiful collection
of technical pieces.
★ **Musée de l'Homme**
(**D** A3)
→ *Palais de Chaillot
17, pl. du Trocadéro (16th)*

*Tel. 01 44 05 72 72
Wed-Mon 9.45am–5.15pm.*
Prehistory, anthropology,
biology and ethnology are
the themes tackled by this
museum (which is part of
the Museum of Natural
History). Weaponry, jewelry
costumes and sculpture are
exhibited by geographical
location and theme.
★ **Tour Eiffel /
Champ-de-Mars** (**D** B4)
→ *Champ-de-Mars (7th)
Summer: daily 9am–midnight
Winter: daily 9.30am–11pm.*
The symbol of Paris, it was
erected in 1889 for the
World Exhibition. The Eiffel
Tower was, at that time, the
tallest building in Paris.

Now, including the anten
on the top, this gigantic
steel structure stands
1,053 ft high. From the to
floor observatory, you ca
see for 40 miles across
Paris on a clear day. But i
is from the base that you
get a real sense of its
magnitude. At the foot of
the tower, the Champ- de-
Mars park, (designed in
1908), stretches all the w
to the l'École Militaire.
From there you get a
stunning view of the Eiffe
Tower and the Trocadéro.
★ **Palais de Tokyo /
Musée d'Art Moderne
la Ville de Paris** (**D** B2)
→ *11, ave. Président-Wilso*

D

ARC DE TRIOMPHE

TROCADÉRO

MUSÉE DE L'HOMME

Map labels

AVENUE FOCH

ARC DE TRIOMPHE ★

R. CHAT.

OFFICE TOURISME

AIR FRANCE

GEOR

R. DE PRESBOURG

KLÉBER Ⓜ

AVENUE VICTOR-HUGO

RUE PAUL-VALERY

RUE LAURISTON

RUE DE LA PÉROUSE

AVENUE D'IÉNA

AVENUE MARCEAU

RUE GALILÉE

RUE VERNET

CENTRE DE CONFÉRENCES INTERNATIONALES

RUE LAURISTON

AVENUE KLÉBER

RUE GALILÉE

RUE GIRAUDOUX

RUE BASSANO

RUE QUE

RUE COPERNIC

Pl. des États-Unis

BOISSIÈRE Ⓜ

XVIe

RUE DE CHAILLOT

AVENUE MARCEAU

SERBIE

RUE BOISSIÈRE

RUE LAURISTON

R. LÉO-DELIBES

RUE BOISSIÈRE

AVENUE KLÉBER

RUE DE LUBECK

AVENUE D'IÉNA

AMER CATHE IN PA

RUE ST-DIDIER

AV. PIERRE-1er DE-

MUSÉE GUIMET

PALAIS GALLIERA

ALI

RUE DE LONGCHAMP

IÉNA Ⓜ

PRÉSIDENT-WILSON

AVENUE DU Place d'Iéna

IÉNA Ⓜ

TROCADÉRO Ⓜ

MUSÉE DE LA MARINE ★

PALAIS DE TOKYO MUSÉE D'ART MODERNE ★

Ⓜ Place du Trocadéro-et du-11-Novembre Ⓜ

RUE FRESNEL

PASSERELLE DEBILLY

NATIONS-UNIES

MUSÉE DE L'HOMME ★

AVENUE DE NEW YORK

S E I N E

PONT D

R

TROCADÉRO ★

Place de Varsovie

BRANLY

RUE DE L'UNIVERSITÉ

AVENUE DES

PONT D'IÉNA

RUE DE MONTTESSUY

AVENUE

RUE

AVENUE

TOUR EIFFEL CHAMP-DE-MARS ★

DE LA

CHAMP-DE-MARS (R.E.R.) Ⓜ

AV.

AV. GUSTAVE-EIFFEL

GÉNÉRAL-FERRIÉ

Pl. du Gal Gouraud

ERITE

ERITE

From La Concorde, the Champs-Élysées is an unforgettable sight. The famous throughfare stretches majestically to the Arc de Triomphe. Restaurants, cafés, chic night-clubs and even expensive car show-rooms draw a colorful crowd day and night. Avenue Montaigne, the epitome of luxury and home to Chanel, Christian Dior, Louis Vuitton, Nina Ricci and Christian Lacroix, the best couturiers and designers, descends toward the Seine. Les Invalides and the Champ-de-Mars stretch along the opposite bank, lined with lovely townhouses and offering impressive views of the Eiffel Tower.

APOLLON   CAFÉ THOUMIEUX

RESTAURANTS

Apollon (**D** C3)
→ 24, rue Jean-Nicot (7th)
Tel. 01 45 55 68 47
Last orders 11pm; closed Sun.
A tiny restaurant full of Mediterranean color. Cheese from Cyprus, basil, feta and tomato salads, *souvlakis* (kebabs), ground-rice cake with lemon zest. Lunch menu 85F.

L'Ami-Jean (**D** C3)
→ 27, rue Malar (7th)
Tel. 01 47 05 86 89
Closed Sun.
The photos hanging on the walls tell you that you have entered Basque country. Friendly service with an eclectic clientele. The south-west French cuisine includes: magret of duck, Spanish omelette, and Basque gâteau. Daily specials 74–92F; à la carte 180F, set menu 99F.

Noura (**D** B2)
→ 21–27, ave. Marceau (16th) Tel. 01 47 23 02 20
Daily until midnight.
One of the best Lebanese restaurants in Paris. Plates of *meze* at 68F, *chawarma* chicken-tabouleh 84F and pastries 24F. Excellent wine list, all available by the glass.

Le Bistrot de Marius Rive Gauche (**D** D4)
→ 74, bd de la Tour-Maubourg (7th)
Tel. 01 47 53 80 86
Daily noon–2.30pm, 7–10.30pm.
This is one of the best fish restaurants in Paris: very fresh produce and simple, delicious dishes. Even better: it is open on Sun. Entrées 48F, main course up to 145F, desserts c.38F.

Tampopo (**D** A2)
→ 66, rue Lauriston (16th)
Tel. 01 47 27 74 52
Closed Sat lunch and Sun.
Nothing like the hectic Japanese restaurants on Rue Ste-Anne. Here you remove your shoes at the door and step into an atmosphere of zen calm and serenity; ancient traditions of Japanese cooking. Set menus 90F and 120F at lunchtime, 150F dinner.

La Fermette Marbeuf 1900 (**D** C2)
→ 5, rue Marbeuf (8th)
Tel. 01 53 23 08 00
Daily noon–3pm, 7pm–midnight.
Gilbert Isaac's excellent kitchen serves traditional cooking in a stunning Art-Nouveau décor. Pleasant terrace and a truly good wine list. Set menu 180F.

CHRISTIAN LACROIX

CHANEL

FAGUAIS

La Maison de l'Alsace (D C1)

→ 39, ave. des Champs-Élysées (8th)
Tel. 01 53 93 97 00
Daily 24 hours.
This large brasserie on Champs-Élysées never closes and serves some of the best Alsatian food in Paris. Saueurkraut, roasted suckling pig, incredibly fresh seafood platters. À la carte 250F.

TEAROOMS

Ladurée (D C1)

→ 75, ave. des Champs-Élysées (8th)
Tel. 01 40 75 08 75
Daily 7.30am–10m.
Thirty flavors of macaroons including coffee, chocolate, vanilla, rose petal and Guérande caramel. All served against a backdrop of stucco, gilt and marble. Genteel service.
The other Ladurée is at 16, rue Royale (8th). 18F large macaroon, 7.50F small.

CAFÉS, BARS, MUSIC VENUES

Café du Musée Rodin (D D4)

→ 77, rue de Varenne (7th)
Tel. 01 45 50 42 34 Tue-

Sun 10am–6pm (4.30pm in winter).
Enjoy a pleasant drink or snack in the tranquil setting of the Rodin Museum statue garden. Entrance fee to the garden 5F.

Café Thoumieux (D C3)

→ 4, rue de la Comète (7th) Tel. 01 45 51 50 40
Mon-Fri noon–2am;
Sat 7pm–2am.
Red velvet décor enjoyed by a young sophisticated clientele. Excellent cocktails 50F, tapas 60F and a huge screen showing sports events.

Master's Bar (D C4)

→ 64, ave. Bosquet (7th)
Tel. 01 45 51 08 99
Daily 5pm–2am.
Thierry Delamare's famous cocktails. Happy hour during the week from 5–7pm. Cocktails 48–58F.

Le Doobie's (D C2)

→ 2, rue Robert-Estienne (8th) Tel. 01 53 76 10 76
Mon-Sat 6pm–2am;
Sun noon–2am.
A favorite with the fashion set. Cozy and intimate. Cocktails 60F.

Au Dernier Métro (D A5)

→ 70, bd de Grenelle (15th)
Tel. 01 45 75 01 23
Daily 6am–2am.
A bar in a colorful

quartier where you can choose between 10 different draught beers alongside friends and locals. Lively atmosphere, especially on soccer match nights! Excellent south-west French cuisine. Main course 58–90F.

Le Queen (D C1)

→ 102, ave. des Champs-Élysées (8th)
Tel. 01 53 89 08 90
Daily midnight–dawn.
This major club is one of the best Parisian gay bars. Erotic dancing for men only on Thursday and Saturday.
Themed nights: 'Disco' (Mon), 'Private' (Tue), 'Secret' (Wed), 'French variety' (Thu), 'House' (Fri-Sat) and '1980-90s' (Sun).

Théâtre des Champs-Élysées (D C2)

→ 15, ave. Montaigne (8th)
Tel. 01 49 52 50 50
Mon-Sat. Closed July–Aug.
Opera, lyric opera, chamber music (on Sundays the Orchestre National de France) and contemporary dance under the direction of Dominique Meyer. Tickets 40–450F.
The theater's rooftop restaurant, Maison Blanche '15 Montaigne' offers gastronomic food

and a breathtaking view of Paris.

SHOPPING

La Maison du Chocolat (D C1)

→ 56, rue Pierre-Charron (8th) Tel. 01 47 23 38 25
Mon-Sat 10am–7.30pm.
Chocolate in all possible forms: macaroons, chocolate bars, candies, drinks, pastries ... Heaven on earth for chocoholics.

Faguais (D C2)

→ 30, rue de La Trémoille (8th) Tel. 01 47 20 80 91
Mon-Sat 9.30am–7pm.
Traditional-style grocery store. More than 2,000 kinds of produce made by traditional methods: Montélimar nougat, Agen prunes, Calissons d'Aix (almond paste sweets), teas, preserves and 50 rare coffee blends.

Virgin Mega store (D C1)

→ 52, ave. des Champs-Élysées (8th)
Tel. 49 53 50 00
Mon-Sat 10am–midnight, Sun and public holidays noon–midnight.
In a lovely 1930s building: books, music, videos and on the top floor the Virgin Café, where you can grab a bite to eat or just stop for a drink. Daily specials 50–60F, à la carte 150F.

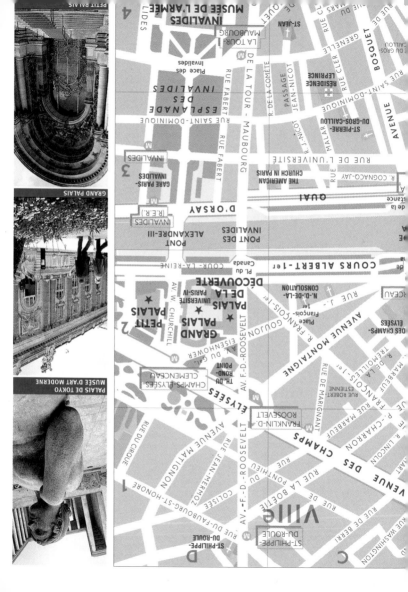

PETIT PALAIS

GRAND PALAIS

PALAIS DE TOKYO
MUSÉE D'ART MODERNE

MUSÉE DE L'ARMÉE
INVALIDES 4

LA TOUR-
MAUBOURG

Place des
Invalides

ESPLANADE
DES
INVALIDES

RUE FABERT

RUE DE LA TOUR-MAUBOURG

RUE DE GRENELLE

RUE CLER

RUE DU
CHAMP DE MARS

RUE DE GRENELLE

AVENUE BOSQUET

RUE DU GROS-
CAILLOU

RUE SAINT-DOMINIQUE

RÉSIDENCE
LEPRINCE

RUE CLER

RUE-DE-LA-COMÈTE

R. DE LA COMÈTE

PASSAGE
JEAN-NICOT

RUE SAINT-DOMINIQUE

RUE JEAN-NICOT

RUE MALAR

ST-PIERRE-
DU-GROS-CAILLOU

AVENUE RAPP

GARE PARIS-
INVALIDES

INVALIDES

RUE FABERT

RUE DE L'UNIVERSITÉ

THE AMERICAN
CHURCH IN PARIS

R. COGNACQ-JAY

RUE COGNACQ-JAY

A
de la
stance

QUAI D'ORSAY

INVALIDES
(R.E.R.)

PONT DES
INVALIDES

PONT
ALEXANDRE-III

COURS LA-REINE

Pl. du
Canada

COURS ALBERT-1er

de
la

AE

CEAU

PALAIS
DE LA
DÉCOUVERTE

AV. W. CHURCHILL

GRAND
PALAIS

UNIVERSITÉ
PARIS-IV

EISENHOWER

AV. DU Gal-

R. PONCELET

CHAMPS-ÉLYSÉES-
CLEMENCEAU

TH. DU
ROND-
POINT

PETIT
PALAIS

AV. F.-D.-ROOSEVELT

R. JEAN GOUJON

Place
François-1er

N.-D.-DE-LA-
CONSOLATION

RUE J.-

AVENUE MONTAIGNE

RUE DE MARIGNAN

CHAMPS-
ÉLYSÉES
DES CHAMPS-
ÉLYSÉES

FRANKLIN-D.-
ROOSEVELT

P.-CHARRON

RUE ROBERT-
ESTIENNE

RUE
DE LA
TRÉMOILLE

RUE FRANÇOIS-1er

RUE MARBEUF

RUE DU CIRQUE

RUE JEAN-MERMOZ

RUE DU COLISÉE

AV.- F.-D.-ROOSEVELT

RUE DE PONTHIEU

RUE LA BOÉTIE

RUE MATIGNON

AVENUE DES CHAMPS

VIIIe

RUE DU-FAUBOURG-ST-HONORÉ

ST-PHILIPPE-
DU-ROULE

ST-PHILIPPE-
DU-ROULE

RUE DE BERRI

RUE DE WASHINGTON

R. LINCOLN

RUE WASHINGTON

RUE LINCOLN

AVENUE

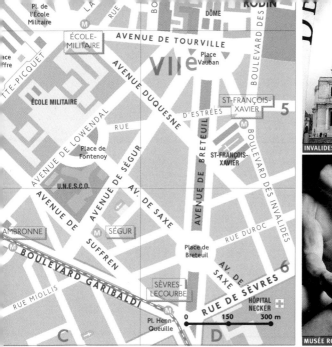

INVALIDES

MUSÉE RODIN

5ʰ) Tel. 01 40 51 38 38
e-Sun 10am–5.30pm.
ened in 1961 inside
e Palais de Tokyo, the
useum of Modern Art of
e City of Paris contains a
perb collection of works
Matisse, Dufy, Braque,
d Picasso. Each year it
s a huge exhibition
sed around a particular
tist or theme.

**Palais de la
écouverte (D** D2)
Ave. Franklin-Roosevelt
ʰ) Tel. 01 56 43 20 21
e-Sat 9.30am–5.30pm;
n 10am–6.30pm.
ively approach to
arning about science via
rious interactive exhibits.

★ **Petit Palais (D** D2)
→ 1, ave. Winston-Churchill
(8ᵗʰ) Tel. 01 42 65 12 73
Tue-Sun 10am–5.40pm.
Home to Paris' Beaux-Arts
Museum (closed until
2002) and a site for large
temporary exhibitions.

★ **Grand Palais (D** D2)
→ Ave. Winston-Churchill
(8ᵗʰ) Tel. 01 44 13 17 17
Wed 10am–10pm;
Thu-Mon 10am–8pm.
The Grand Palais, partially
closed for building work,
houses large temporary art
exhibitions.

★ **Invalides/Musée
de l'Armée (D** D4)
→ Esplanade des Invalides
(5ᵗʰ) Tel. 01 44 42 37 67

Daily 10am–6pm (5pm in
winter).
The golden dome can be
seen for miles. Built for
Louis XIV in 1671-6, the
building served as a
hospital for the wounded
king's soldiers. Today the
Invalides contains the
Musée de l'Ordre de la
Libération, the church of
Saint-Louis and the tomb
of Napoleon I. A large part
of the war museum's
collection consists of
weaponry and items from
the collection of Napoleon
III.

★ **Musée Rodin (D** D4)
→ 77, rue de Varenne (7ᵗʰ)
Tel. 01 44 18 61 10

Tue-Sun 9.30am–4.45pm
(3.45pm in winter).
One of the most appealing
museums in Paris, this was
once Rodin's home and
workshop. It was converted
into a museum two years
after his death. Around
500 sculptures and 8000
photographs and drawings
by the artist are exhibited
here by rotation. Some of
Rodin's most important
works, including Le
Penseur (The Thinker), La
Porte de l'enfer (The Gates
of Hell) and Les Bourgeois
de Calais (The Burghers of
Calais) are on display in the
garden, under the shade of
the lime trees.

ÉGLISE SAINT-PIERRE

PLACE DU TERTRE

★ Cimetière de Montmartre (E A3)

→ 20, ave. Rachel (18th)
Tel. 01 43 87 64 24
Daily 9am–5.45pm
The undulating country-side, the 100-year-old trees and the beautiful statues are all reminiscent of the Père-Lachaise cemetery. In this romantic setting lie the remains of, among others, Berlioz, Offenbach, Zola Fragonard, Vigny, Sacha Guitry, A. Dumas, Nijinsky and François Truffaut. Thirteen years after her death, flowers and poems are still left every day on the tomb of the singer Dalida who lived nearby.

★ Musée de Montmartre (E C3)

→ 12, rue Cortot (18th)
Tel. 01 46 06 61 11
Tue–Sun 11am–5.30pm.
A complete history of the quartier (cabarets, painters and singers) told via posters, paintings, music and photographs. Housed in a charming 17th-century house overlooking the vineyards.

★ Sacré-Cœur (E C3)

→ 35, rue du Chevalier-de-La-Barre (18th)
Tel. 01 53 41 89 00
Daily 6am–11pm.
Symbol of la Butte and of a Paris now long gone, this church with its Romanesque-Byzantine silhouette is an integral part of the Montmartre landscape. It was declared a public utility by the Chamber of Deputies from 1875 to 1919. It offers the best views of Paris (from the steps and from the dome itself).

★ Église Saint-Pierre-de-Montmartre (E C3)

→ 2, rue du Mont-Cenis (18th) Tel. 01 46 06 57 63
Mon–Sat 8.30am–7.30pm (6.30pm Sun).
One of the oldest churches in Paris, hidden behind an 18th-century façade. This is all that now remains of the Abbaye aux Dames (1147), erected on what are presumed to be the remains of an ancient Gallo-Roman temple; the four marble columns in the choir probably date from this time. Beneath the choir and the transept lies the tombstone of its founder, Queen Adélaïde.

★ Place du Tertre (E C

Street artists specializing in portraits or caricatures a mass of easels, flocks tourists ... this former square of the old village has become a Montmart cliché. But in the early morning when the squa is at its quietest, it is ver pleasant to have coffee

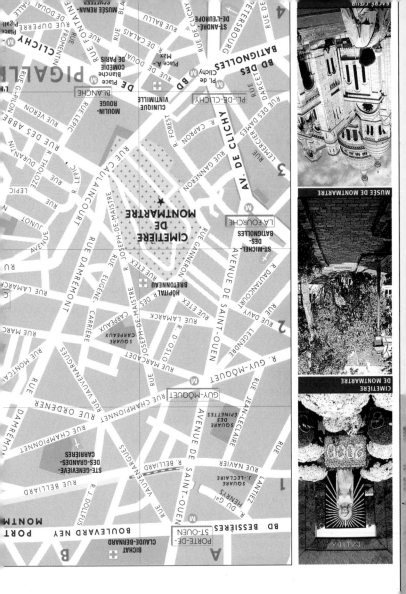

MUSÉE DE MONTMARTRE

CIMETIÈRE DE MONTMARTRE

DALIDA

The Sacré-Cœur, perched at the top of La Butte, attracts tourists from all over the world. The artists, cabarets and balls of the Belle Époque may be long gone but the old charm of Montmartre lives on in the steep streets, stairways and pretty, ivy-covered houses. As evening falls the concert halls on the boulevards fill up and the sex scene in Pigalle begins to come to life. Two minutes away the Nouvelle Athène entices visitors with the romantic charm of its quiet little streets and Directoire-style architecture – an oasis in the midst of the bustle of the big boulevards.

BOUILLON CHARTIER

L'ÉTÉ EN PENTE DOUCE

RESTAURANTS

Le Zouave Gobichon (E B3)
→ 8, rue Durantin (18th) Tel. 01 46 06 25 75 Closed Sun lunch and Mon. Small, cozy dining room serving good quality, varied French cuisine. Zouave often invites local artists to exhibit their works here. Vegetarian special 69F.

L'Été en Pente Douce (E B2)
→ 23, rue Muller (18th) Tel. 01 42 64 02 67. Daily. Restaurant and tearoom with a large terrace. Salads 48–56F, traditional dishes 72–95F. Seasonal and vegetarian menus.

Bouillon Chartier (E C6)
→ 7, rue du Faubourg-Montmartre (9th) Tel. 01 47 70 86 29. Daily 11.30am–3pm, 6–10pm. Superb Belle Époque canteen serving cheap, straightforward cooking in the midst of a pleasant hubbub. Set menu 78F.

Le Mono (E B3)
→ 40, rue Véron (18th) Tel. 01 46 06 99 20 Mon-Tue and Thu-Sun 7–11.30pm (lunch by reservation). Typical décor, music and food from Togo. Specialties include: gbekui (smoked fish in spinach sauce), chicken djenkoumé (half wheat, half corn-meal pastry) and braised fish in moyo (mild spices). À la carte 100F.

Per Bacco (E D3)
→ 10, rue Lambert (18th) Tel. 01 42 52 22 40 Mon-Fri noon–2.30pm, 8–10.30pm; Sat 8–10.30pm. The Naples-born chef of this restaurant has his produce sent direct from Italy. Authentic cuisine in an unpretentious setting. Attentive service. À la carte 200F.

Beauvilliers (E C2)
→ 52, rue Lamarck (18th) Tel. 01 42 54 54 42. Closed Sun and Mon lunch. The most prestigious restaurant on la Butte, run by maître d' Édouard Carlier. Elegantly imaginative gastronomy: grilled red mullet in fine escabèche (marinaded and served cold), artichoke hearts stuffed with crab. Set menu 185F lunch, 400F dinner (including wine).

BARS, CLUBS, CABARET

Le Sancerre (E B3)
→ 35, rue des Abbesses (18th) Tel. 01 42 58 08 20 This trendy café-bar is

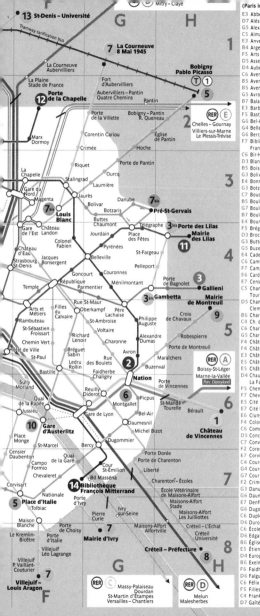

St-Denis – Université 13

Tramway tarification bus

La Courneuve 8 Mai 1945 7

La Courneuve Aubervilliers

La Plaine Stade de France

Porte de la Chapelle 12

Bobigny Pablo Picasso (T) (1)

Fort d'Aubervilliers 5

Marx Dormoy

La Chapelle

Aubervilliers – Pantin Quatre Chemins

Porte de la Villette

Bobigny – Pantin R. Queneau

Pantin

Corentin Cariou

Église de Pantin

Crimée

Hoche

Gare du Nord

Stalingrad

Riquet

Porte de Pantin

Magenta

Jaurès

Ourcq

Laumière

Louis Blanc 7bis

Bolivar

Danube 7bis

Pré-St-Gervais

Château Landon

Buttes Chaumont

Jourdain

Télégraphe

Gare de l'Est

Colonel Fabien

Pyrénées

Place des Fêtes

Porte des Lilas 3bis

Mairie des Lilas 11

Château d'Eau

Strasbourg St-Denis

Jacques Bonsergent

Belleville

St-Fargeau

Temple

République

Goncourt

Parmentier

Couronnes

Pelleport

Arts et Métiers

Filles du Calvaire

Rue St-Maur

Oberkampf

Père Lachaise

Ménilmontant

Porte de Bagnolet 3

Gallieni 3

Rambuteau

St-Sébastien Froissart

Richard Lenoir

Voltaire

Croix de Chavaux

Gambetta 3bis

Mairie de Montreuil

Chemin Vert

Bréguet Sabin

Philippe Auguste

Alexandre Dumas

Robespierre

Porte de Montreuil

9

Hôtel de Ville

St-Paul

Ledru Rollin

Rue des Boulets

Avron

Bastille

Faidherbe Chaligny

Buzenval

Nation 2

Porte de Vincennes

Sully Morland

Quai de la Rapée

Jussieu

Reuilly Diderot

Gare de Lyon 6

Montgallet

Picpus

St-Mandé Tourelle

Bérault

1

Place Monge

Gare d'Austerlitz 10

Daumesnil

Bel-Air

Michel Bizet

Bercy

Dugommier

Château de Vincennes

St-Marcel

Quai de la Gare

Cour St-Émilion

Porte Dorée

Censier Daubenton

Campo Formio

Bercy

Liberté

Chevaleret

Nationale

Corvisart

Cour St-Émilion

Charenton–Écoles

Bibliothèque François Mitterrand 14

École Vétérinaire de Maisons-Alfort

Place d'Italie 5

Tolbiac

Porte d'Ivry

Maison Blanche

Porte de Choisy 7

Maisons-Alfort Stade

Maisons-Alfort Les Juilliottes

Créteil–L'Échat

Le Kremlin-Bicêtre

Mairie d'Ivry 7

Villejuif Léo Lagrange

Pierre Curie

Ivry-sur-Seine

Maisons-Alfort Alfortville

Créteil Université

Villejuif P. Vaillant-Couturier 7

Créteil – Préfecture 8

Villejuif – Louis Aragon 7

(RER) (C) Massy-Palaiseau Dourdan St-Martin d'Étampes Versailles – Chantiers

(RER) (D) Melun Malesherbes

(RER) (E) Chelles – Gournay Villiers-sur-Marne Le Plessis-Trévise

(RER) (A) Boissy-St-Léger Marne-la-Vallée Parc Disneyland

Mitry – Claye

(Paris intra-muros) :

E3 Abbesses
D7 Alésia
G5 Alexandre Dumas
C5 Alma – Marceau
E3 Anvers
F5 Arts et Métiers
D5 Assemblée Nationale
D4 Auber
B5 Avenue Émile Zola
B5 Avenue Foch
B5 Avenue Henri Martin
G5 Avron
E3 Balard
E3 Barbès-Rochechouart
G5 Bastille
G5 Bel-Air
C6 Belleville
C7 Bercy
F Bibliothèque François Mitterrand
D3 Bir-Hakeim
D3 Blanche
E4 Boissière
D3 Bolivar
E4 Bonne Nouvelle
C7 Botzaris
C7 Boucicaut
G7 Boulainvilliers
G7 Boulevard Masséna
G7 Boulevard Victor
E4 Bourse
F3 Bréguet – Sabin
F3 Brochant
G3 Buttes Chaumont
G5 Buzenval
C6 Cambronne
E7 Campo-Formio
E6 Cardinal Lemoine
E7 Censier – Daubenton
C5 Champ de Mars Tour Eiffel
E5 Champs-Élysées Clemenceau
B6 Chardon-Lagache
C5 Ch. de Gaulle – Étoile
C5 Charles Michels
G5 Charonne
F4 Château d'Eau
F3 Château-Landon
F4 Château Rouge
E5 Châtelet
E5 Châtelet – Les Halles
D4 Chaussée d'Antin La Fayette
F4 Chemin Vert
F7 Chevaleret
E5 Cité
E7 Cité Universitaire
F4 Colonel Fabien
C6 Commerce
E5 Concorde
C7 Convention
F7 Corentin Cariou
F4 Corvisart
C4 Courcelles
G5 Couronnes
G7 Cour St-Émilion
F7 Crimée
G3 Danube
E7 Daumesnil
E7 Denfert-Rochereau
D6 Dugommier
C6 Dupleix
C6 Duroc
C6 École Militaire
D6 Edgar Quinet
B6 Église d'Auteuil
E5 Étienne Marcel
D4 Europe
B5 Exelmans
F6 Faidherbe – Chaligny
D6 Falguière
C6 Félix Faure
F5 Filles du Calvaire
C4 Franklin D. Roosevelt
D7 Gaîté

F4 Gare de l'Est
G5 Gare de Lyon
D6 Gare Montparnasse
E3 Gare du Nord
B5 Gare St-Lazare
C4 George V
F4 Glacière
F4 Goncourt
E4 Grands Boulevards
D2 Guy Môquet
D4 Haussmann – St-Lazare
D4 Havre – Caumartin
C5 Héna
D5 Invalides
H4 Jacques Bonsergent
B6 Jasmin
F3 Jaurès
B6 Javel – André Citroën
G4 Jourdain
E2 Jules Joffrin
F6 Jussieu
B6 Kennedy – Radio France
B4 Kléber
E3 La Chapelle
D3 La Fourche
E2 Lamarck – Caulaincourt
C6 La Motte-Picquet Grenelle
B5 La Muette
C5 La Tour-Maubourg
G3 Laumière
F5 Ledru-Rollin
E7 Le Peletier
E7 Les Gobelins
E5 Les Halles
D3 Liège ♦
E7 Louis Blanc
C7 Lourmel
E6 Louvre – Rivoli
E6 Luxembourg
D5 Mabillon
D4 Madeleine
F3 Magenta
F7 Maison Blanche ¼
C3 Malesherbes
H5 Maraîchers
E2 Marcadet – Poissonniers
F2 Marx Dormoy
E6 Maubert – Mutualité
G6 Michel Ange – Auteuil
B6 Michel Ange – Molitor
G6 Michel Bizet
F5 Mirabeau
D4 Miromesnil
G6 Monceau
G6 Montgallet
D6 Montparnasse Bienvenüe
D7 Mouton-Duvernet
D7 Musée d'Orsay
G6 Nation
F7 Nationale
D3 N.-Dame-de-Lorette
D6 N.-Dame-des-Champs
F5 Oberkampf
E6 Odéon
D4 Opéra
D5 Ourcq
D5 Palais Royal Musée du Louvre
F4 Parmentier
B5 Passy
G6 Pasteur
H4 Pelleport
C3 Pereire
C5 Père Lachaise
D7 Pernety
G5 Philippe Auguste
G6 Picpus
E3 Pigalle
D3 Place de Clichy
G4 Place des Fêtes
F7 Place d'Italie
E6 Place Monge
D7 Plaisance
E4 Poissonnière
C5 Pont de l'Alma
E5 Pont Marie

A6 Pte d'Auteuil
H4 Pte de Bagnolet
C3 Pte de Champerret
G7 Pte de Charenton
F7 Pte de Choisy
D2 Pte de Clichy
E2 Pte de Clignancourt
F2 Pte de la Chapelle
G2 Pte de la Villette
H5 Pte de Montreuil
G3 Pte de Pantin
A7 Pte de St-Cloud
D2 Pte de St-Ouen
H4 Pte des Lilas
D7 Pte de Vanves
C7 Pte de Versailles
H6 Pte de Vincennes
F2 Pte d'Italie
F7 Pte d'Ivry
G7 Pte Dorée
D7 Pte d'Orléans
B4 Pte Maillot
E6 Port-Royal
G3 Pré-St-Gervais
G5 Pyramides
G4 Pyrénées
F7 Quai de la Gare
G6 Quai de la Rapée
E4 Quatre Septembre
F5 Rambuteau
B5 Ranelagh
D7 Raspail
F2 Réaumur – Sébastopol
D6 Rennes ♦
F4 République
G6 Reuilly – Diderot
F5 Richard-Lenoir
E4 Richelieu – Drouot
F3 Riquet
F2 Rome
B5 Rue de la Pompe
G6 Rue des Boulets
D5 Rue du Bac
G4 Rue St-Maur
C5 St-Ambroise
D4 St-Augustin
H4 St-Fargeau
D5 St-François-Xavier
E3 St-Georges
D6 St-Germain-des-Prés
E5 St-Jacques
D4 St-Lazare
F6 St-Marcel
E6 St-Michel
E6 St-Michel Notre-Dame
F5 St-Paul
C4 St-Philippe-du-Roule
F5 St-Placide
F5 St-Sébastien Froissart
D6 St-Sulpice
C6 Ségur
E4 Sentier
C6 Sèvres – Babylone
C6 Sèvres – Lecourbe
E2 Simplon
D3 Solférino
F3 Stalingrad
E4 Strasbourg St-Denis
F6 Sully – Morland
G4 Télégraphe
F4 Temple
F7 Ternes
F7 Tolbiac
D3 Trinité d'Estienne d'Orves
B5 Trocadéro
D5 Tuileries
D6 Vaneau
D5 Varenne
C6 Vaugirard
D6 Vavin
B5 Victor Hugo
C3 Volontaires
G5 Voltaire
C3 Wagram

THE NEWLY OPENED LINE 14: MÉTÉOR

Métro
16 lines (numbered from 1–14) within Paris and the nearby suburbs (zones 1–2).
→ *Daily 5.30am–12.30am*

RER
5 fast trains (A, B, C, D, E) across Paris and the Île-de-France (zones 1–8).
→ *Daily 5.30am–12.30am*

RATP trains
The regional network is divided into 5 zones: 1–2 (city center – single fare) and 3–5 (suburbs).

Buses
58 lines. Reduced service Sun and public holidays.
→ *Mon–Fri 5.30am–8.30pm*

Nightbuses
Run from 1am to 5am.

RATP information
→ *Tel. 01 36 68 77 14*

Fares
Tickets for the métro, the RER and buses are available from métro stations (ticket offices and ticket machines) and tobacconists.
→ *8F single ticket, 55F book of 10 (carnet)*

Travel passes
Paris Visite
→ *55–350F depending on the number of days (1, 2, 3 or 5 days) and the zones covered)*
Applies to all modes of transport.
Reduced prices to the monuments of Paris and the surrounding area.

Mobilis
→ *40–110F depending on the zones covered*
Valid for one day only in the relevant zone(s).

---

eption all contribute to charm of the place. ms from 680F with a top view of Paris and Sacré Cœur. Breakfast erved in what used to he dressing rooms of m Juan', a former os cabaret.

tel des Grands mmes (A D3)
l. du Panthéon (5ᵗʰ) 01 46 34 19 60
s elegant 18th-century el has 32 spacious ms with exposed ms and wrought-iron heads. Views of the theon dome from 6th-floor balconies. erve well in adavance. m 750F.

ER 800F

tel des Jardins du xembourg (A C3)
, Impasse Royer-Collar Tel. 01 40 60 08 88
883 Freud stayed here.

This splendid hotel has now been completely renovated in a Provençal style: kilims, wood-paneling, small balconies, flowers and tiling give the rooms an unforgettable charm. The extremely spacious Room 1 even has its own entrance. Sauna, elevator, patio and air-conditioning. From 810F.

Hôtel des Marronniers (A B1)
→ *21, rue Jacob (6ᵗʰ)* Tel. 01 43 25 30 60
A good address. Views of the clocktower of Saint-Germain or the garden from some of the rooms. Breakfast is served on the veranda. From 825F.

PALACES

Hôtel Raphaël (D A1)
→ *17, ave Kléber (16ᵗʰ)* Tel. 01 53 64 32 00
www.raphael-hotel.com
A minute's walk from the

Champs-Élysées, this is probably the smallest but most charming of Parisian palaces. Ninety rooms and suites whose antique furniture is cared for daily by the in-house cabinet-maker. Aubusson tapestries, 18th-century inspired mural paintings, Louis-XV wood paneling, and magnificent views of the Arc de Triomphe from the 7th floor. There, on the biggest and most romantic terrace in Paris, have lunch or just a drink. From 2,700F.
And if a night at the Ritz (tel. 01 43 16 30 30), the Crillon (tel. 01 44 71 15 00), the Plaza-Athénée (tel. 01 53 67 66 65) or the Hôtel Costes (tel. 01 42 44 50 00) is just a dream, why not treat yourself to breakfast there (expect to pay between 200 and 350F). Smart dress required. Book in advance.

MOULIN-ROUGE   PRINTEMPS   ART'S FACTORY

located in the heart of the Abbesses district. At its best in the late afternoon and evening when the terrace is inundated with locals.

La Fourmi (E C5)
→ *74, rue des Martyrs (18ᵗʰ) Tel. 01 42 64 70 35 Daily 8am–2am.*
Café situated at the crossroads of the trendy section of Pigalle, and near La Cigale, the famous concert hall (*La cigale et la fourmi* is one of La Fontaine's *Fables*). Good crowd and a fashionable place to be seen. Ideal for breakfast or a snack (salads, sandwiches and daily specials).

Élysée-Montmartre (E C4)
→ *72, bd Rochechouart (18ᵗʰ) Tel. 01 55 07 06 00*
Originally a ballroom (1807) this has become a leading light on the Paris dance scene. Fans of alternative rock or world music sway under the 1900s molding. Live band and DJ every other Sat.

Divan du Monde (E C5)
→ *75, rue des Martyrs (18ᵗʰ) Tel. 01 44 92 77 66*
World music (African, Brazilian, Caribbean, Oriental) and also themed evenings, films

and dance in this former Belle Époque cabaret venue.

Rex Club (E D6)
→ *5, bd Poissonnière (2ⁿᵈ) Tel. 01 42 36 10 96 Wed-Sat 11am–dawn.*
Parisian home of electronic music presided over by the best DJs of the moment.

Moulin-Rouge (E B4)
→ *82, bd de Clichy (18ᵗʰ) Tel. 01 53 09 82 82 Daily 7pm (dinner); 9pm, 10pm, (shows).*
A Paris institution! Reservation essential.

Max Linder (E C6)
→ *24, bd Poissonnière (9ᵗʰ) Tel. 01 48 24 00 47*
1930s Art-Deco cinema. Large screen, state-of-the-art sound system and a bar on the ground floor.

SHOPPING

Art's Factory (E C4)
→ *48, rue d'Orsel (18ᵗʰ) Tel. 01 53 28 13 50 Tue-Sat 11am–7.30pm; Sun 2–7pm.*
Dynamic art gallery exhibiting – and selling – contemporary works (paintings, sculpture, photos, objects etc.). Their mission is to promote 'Cheap Art', art which is within everyone's price range.

Patricia Louisor (E C4)
→ *16, rue Houdon (18ᵗʰ) Tel. 01 42 62 10 42 Daily noon–8pm.*
Young stylist in the heart of the fashionable square delineated by Pigalle-Abbesses-Anvers. Fashion that is imaginative, original and also affordable.

Pain d'Épice (E C6)
→ *29 passage Jouffroy (2ⁿᵈ) Tel. 01 47 70 08 68 Mon 12.30–7pm; Tue-Sun 10am–7pm.*
A most amazing toy store. Ancient dolls, accessories for children's parties, wooden mobiles, cots, trains, miniature soldiers and collectors' items.

Department stores (E A6)

Le Printemps
→ *64, bd Haussmann (9ᵗʰ) Mon-Sat 9.35am–7pm (until 10pm Thu).*

Les Galeries Lafayette
→ *40, bd Haussmann (9ᵗʰ) Mon-Sat 9.30am–6.45pm (until 9pm Thu).*
The two best department stores on the Boulevard. Printemps boasts stucco, Belle Époque, Art Deco, and listed 19th-century glass. Top brand names, accessories and an astonishing range of services. Lafayette Gourmet, next door,

is a favorite with foodies and wine lovers. Grab a bite there (tastings every lunchtime) or take out.

Tati (E D4)
→ *4, bd Rochechouart (18ᵗʰ) Tel. 01 55 29 50 00 Mon–Sat 10am–7pm. www.tati.fr*
Open in 1948, this is the first of the Tati stores. 'The lowest prices' in town and guaranteed entertainment!

Marché St-Pierre (E C3)
→ *2, rue Charles-Nodier (18ᵗʰ) Tel. 01 46 06 92 25 Mon 1.30–6.30pm; Wed-Sat 10am–6.30pm.*
Truly the best place to buy fabric, attracting sewing enthusiasts, designers and interior decorators. Over a 2,400-sq-yds area flannel, tweed, silk, linen, cotton, ticking, sequined and floral fabrics sold by the meter.

Puces de Saint-Ouen et Clignancourt (E C1)
→ *Porte de Clignancourt (18ᵗʰ) Sat-Mon 9.30am–7pm*
The oldest and largest of Parisian flea markets: 2,000 outlets, 9 miles to walk and 150,000 visitors each week! Bric-à-brac and specialist markets: Biron (antiques), Malik (fashion), Malassis (art), Serpette (second-hand goods) ...

HALLE SAINT-PIERRE

LA NOUVELLE ATHÈNES

MUSÉE GUSTAVE MOREAU

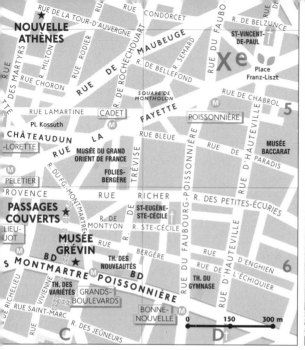

RUE DE LA TOUR-D'AUVERGNE — RUE CONDORCET — RUE DU FAUBO... — R. DE BELZUNCE

NOUVELLE ATHÈNES ★

ST-VINCENT-DE-PAUL

RUE RODIER — RUE DE ROCHECHOUART — MAUBEUGE — RUE DU FAUB... — R. DE BELZUNCE

Xe

Place Franz-Liszt

R. MILTON — RUE DE BELLEFOND — R. SEMARD

RUE CHORON — SQUARE DE MONTHOLON — RUE DE CHABROL

RUE DES MARTYRS — LA RUE — FAYETTE — POISSONNIÈRE — 5

RUE LAMARTINE — CADET Ⓜ

Pl. Kossuth

CHÂTEAUDUN — RUE BLEUE — RUE DE HAUTEVILLE — MUSÉE BACCARAT

-LORETTE — RUE — MUSÉE DU GRAND ORIENT DE FRANCE — RUE DE PARADIS

Ⓜ PELETIER — FOLIES-BERGÈRE — RUE DU FG-MONTMARTRE — RUE DE TRÉVISE — RUE DES POISSONNIÈRE

PROVENCE — RUE — RICHER — R. DES PETITES-ÉCURIES

PASSAGES COUVERTS ★ — ST-EUGÈNE-STE-CÉCILE — R. DE MONTYON — R. STE-CÉCILE

LIEU-OT Ⓜ — RUE — BERGÈRE — RUE D'ENGHIEN — 6

MUSÉE GRÉVIN ★ — TH. DES NOUVEAUTÉS — RUE DU FAUBOURG-POISSONNIÈRE — RUE DE L'ÉCHIQUIER

BD MONTMARTRE ★ — POISSONNIÈRE BD

TH. DES VARIÉTÉS — GRANDS-BOULEVARDS — TH. DU GYMNASE — RUE D'HAUTEVILLE

RUE VIVIENNE — RUE SAINT-MARC — DE RICHELIEU

BONNE-NOUVELLE Ⓜ

R. DES JEÛNEURS

0 — 150 — 300 m

C — D

MUSÉE GRÉVIN

PASSAGE JOUFFROY

---

e terrace of La Mère atherine, a bistro which as already popular during e time of the French evolution.

La Nouvelle Athènes
E C4)
he triangle formed by ace Pigalle/Notre-Dame-e-Lorette/Sainte-Trinité as built in the 18th entury and is full of mantic splendor: nglish gardens, court-rds, vaulted passage-ays, and neoclassical uildings where a presti-ous community of artists nce lived and worked erlioz, Sand, Degas, hopin, Dumas...).

★ **Halle Saint-Pierre**
(**E** C3)
→ 2, rue Ronsard (18th)
Tel. 01 42 58 72 89
Daily 10am–6pm.
Small glass and iron-covered marketplace dating from 1868. Since 1986 it has housed the Musée d'Art Naïf Max-Fourny which exhibits primitive art by artists from all over the world. Pleasant tearoom on the ground floor.

★ **Musée Gustave-Moreau** (**E** B5)
→ 14, rue de La Rochefoucauld (9th)
Tel. 01 48 74 38 50
Mon & Wed 11am–5.15pm;
Thu–Sun 10am–12.45pm,

2–5.15pm.
Around 5,000 drawings and 1,200 paintings by the Symbolist painter Gustave Moreau (including *Jupiter et Sémélé*) on show in his former mansion-studio, which was turned into a museum in 1902.

★ **Musée Grévin** (**E** C6)
→ 10, bd Montmartre (9th)
Tel. 01 47 70 85 05
Daily 1–6.30pm (from 10am during school holidays).
Several hundred celebrities, influential and historical figures immortalized as waxworks. This museum, was opened in 1882 by journalist Arthur Meyer and caricaturist Alfred Grévin.

★ **Covered Walkways**
(**E** C6)
→ *Jouffroy, Verdeau and the Panoramas passageways 10–11, bd Montmartre (2nd)*
It took architectural sleight of hand to build this superb series of glass-covered passageways and conceal the irregularities of the site. Panoramas opened in 1799, followed by Jouffroy and Verdeau in 1846 and 1847. The various stores have changed very little. Some of the shop windows are almost miniature museums in their own right filled with books, comics, toys, old cameras ... plus tearooms and restaurants. A gem.

COUR DE L'ÉTOILE-D'OR

COUR DU BEL-AIR

★ **Cimetière du Père-Lachaise** (**F** F2)
→ 16, rue du Repos (19th)
Tel. 01 55 25 82 10 Daily
8am–6pm (5.30pm in winter)
Shaded avenues, under-growth, winding paths, esplanades... this cemetery (1804) is like a miniature world. At bends in the path stand the most extravagant of tombs. Pyramids and Greek temples stand alongside more modest burial sites. Edith Piaf, Paul Eluard, Frédéric Chopin, Honoré de Balzac, Molière and Jim Morrison among others, rest in this fascinating garden of the dead.

★ **Cirque d'Hiver** (**F** B1)
→ 110, rue Amelot (11th)
Tel. 01 47 00 28 81
This extremely beautiful and colorful circus, built by Hittorff and opened by Napoleon III in 1852, has had an eventful past. Concerts, equestrian acts and even olympic shows have taken place here. Acquired by the Bouglione brothers in 1934, it has since been partially returned to its original purpose.

★ **Boulevard Richard-Lenoir** (**F** B2)
At the port of Arsenal, the canal enters into a long tunnel, surfacing a mile

further, level with Rue du Faubourg-du-Temple. In 1859 Haussmann decided to build a platform over the canal and 15 little squares. Renovation work between 1993 and 1996 gave birth to a succession of gardens, fountains and contemporary-style playgrounds. On Thursdays and Sundays a wonderful food market is held between Place de la Bastille and Bréguet-Sabin métro.

★ **Place de la Bastille** (**F** B3)
The storming of this 14th-century fortress caused this square, in the course

of the 19th century, to become the symbol of the French Revolution. At its center, the July column stands in homage to the victims of the *Trois Glorieuses* (the three-day Revolution of July 1830). The walkways of the Opéra district and the numerous terraced bars all around the square are always bustling.

★ **Port de l'Arsenal** (**F** B
Since 1983, the Bassin ha housed an attractive port which each year sees 1,300 vessels pass through. On the east ban a terraced garden stretch from the Bastille to the

F

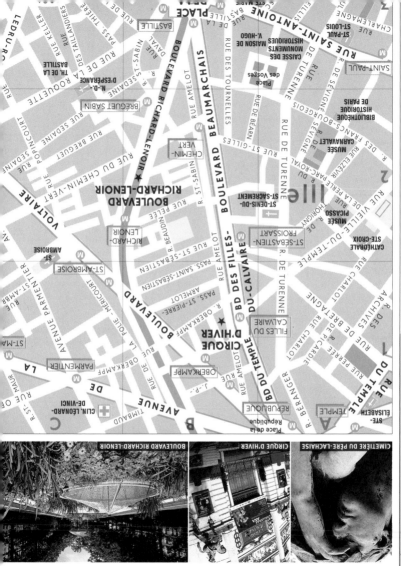

Place de la Bastille is where the capital's dedicated nightlife begins. Cafés, bars and restaurants line the surrounding streets: Rue du Faubourg-St-Antoine, Rue de la Roquette, Rue de Lappe and Rue de Charonne. But carry on further west along the Rue du Faubourg-St-Antoine and take a peek at the maze of courtyards and passageways. Cabinet-makers, for whom this area is renowned, now live alongside designers, architects, graphic designers and stylists. The Oberkampf area, north of Bastille, has now become the hippest, trendiest place to hang out in Paris, attracting nightowls on the prowl for new haunts.

LES AMOGNES

JACQUES MÉLAC

RESTAURANTS

Paris Main d'Or (F C3)
→ *133, rue du Faubourg-Saint-Antoine (11th)
Tel. 01 44 68 04 68
Mon-Sat noon–3pm,
8–11pm.*
Tasty rustic cooking from Corsica: vegetables stuffed with *broccio* cheese, roast goat with potatoes. Set lunch menu 69F, Corsican specialties à la carte.

L'Ébauchoir (F D4)
→ *45, rue de Cîteaux (12th)
Tel. 01 43 42 49 31
Mon-Sat noon–2.30pm,
8–11pm.*
A restaurant reflecting the local craft industry. Simple but good fare: lentil salad, beef *bourguignon*, crème caramel. 3-course lunch menu (incl. wine) 70F.

La Mère Lachaise (F E1)
→ *78, bd de Ménilmontant (20th) Tel. 01 47 97 61 60
Daily 8am–midnight.*
Subdued décor extending onto the large terrace. On the menu, mixed salads, pies and daily specials.
À la carte 90F.

**Le Square Trousseau
(F** C4)
→ *1, rue Antoine-Vollon (11th) Tel. 01 43 43 06 00
Daily noon–2.30pm,
8–11.30pm.*

This attractive bistro offers straightforward cooking, using the best market produce; it caters to a trendy, chic, local clientele. Excellent wine list. À la carte 200F.

Chez Paul (F C3)
→ *13, rue de Charonne (11th) Tel. 01 47 00 34 57
Daily noon–2.30pm,
7pm–midnight.*
An institution in the quartier, nestled behind the crumbling exterior of an old house in the Rue de Charonne. Seafood salad with *foie gras*, grilled peppered steak.
À la carte 160F.

Les Amognes (F E4)
→ *243, rue du Faubourg-Saint-Antoine (11th)
Tel. 01 43 72 73 05
Mon 7.30–10.30pm;
Tue-Sat noon–2pm, 7.30–10.30pm (until 11pm Sat).*
Fresh marinated sardine tart, sautéed squid with garlic and vegetables, crêpe stuffed with eggplant and cardamon. Thierry Coué's kitchen presents seasonal cooking which is both affordable and of good quality. Set menu 180F.

Chardenoux (F D3)
→ *1, rue Jules Vallès (11th)
Mon-Fri noon–2pm,
8–10pm; Sat 8–10.30pm.*
Shiny moldings and a

LA BAGUE DE KENZA

VIADUC DES ARTS

BO PLASTIC

long counter... an old bistro that will take you back in time. Classic cuisine, complimented by inventive specialties (sweet and sour tarts with spiced *confit* of lamb). À la carte 250F.

Blue Elephant (**F** C3)
➔ *43, rue de la Roquette (11ᵗʰ) Tel. 01 47 00 42 00 Closed Sat lunch.*
A tropical paradise: teak wood paneling, luxuriant greenery, Thaï orchids, a fountain splashing gently in the background. Excellent Thai cuisine. À la carte 250F.

CAFÉS, BARS, OPERA

Jacques Mélac (**F** E3)
➔ *42, rue Léon-Frot (11ᵗʰ) Tel. 01 43 70 59 27 Mon 9am–5pm; Tue-Sat 9am–midnight.*
Vines trail over the front of Chez Mélac. Drinking water here is strongly discouraged! Wine, 20-25F a glass, is accompanied by plates of *charcuterie* from the Aveyron region (55F), cheese from Cantal or a hot dish.

Le Café du Passage (**F** C3)
➔ *12, rue de Charonne (11ᵗʰ) Tel. 01 49 29 97 64 Daily noon–2am.*

English décor. Snacks and excellent wines, whiskies and champagne.

L'Entrepôt (**F** C3)
➔ *14, rue de Charonne (11ᵗʰ) Tel. 01 48 06 57 04 Daily until 2am.*
Iron staircase, sofas, old photographs hanging on the walls and atmospheric music playing in the background.
Cocktails: Happy Hour from 5 till 8.30pm.

Le Lèche-Vin (**F** B3)
➔ *13, rue Daval (11ᵗʰ) Tel. 01 43 55 98 91 Tue-Thu 6pm–1am (until 2am Fri-Sat).*
Religious souvenirs of all sorts – icons of the Virgin Mary, Christ and the saints – along with draught beer, loud music and a young clientele ... The décor even extends to the W.Cs!

Le Café Charbon (**F** C1)
➔ *109, rue Oberkampf (11ᵗʰ) Tel. 01 43 57 55 13 Daily until 2am.*
Industrial-style décor (gas lamps, zinc bar) and a very trendy clientele. À la carte 130F.

Les Couleurs (**F** C1)
➔ *117, rue Saint-Maur (11ᵗʰ) Tel. 01 43 57 95 61 Daily until 2am.*
The look here is resolutely grunge, with non-matching formica

tables and old nicotine-stained walls. Lemon punch all day.

Le Balajo (**F** C3)
➔ *9, rue de Lappe (11ᵗʰ) Tel. 01 47 00 07 87 Wed-Sun.*
Opened in 1936, the 'Bal à Jo' revives the tradition of the tea dance, with live accordion music every Thursday and Sunday. There are classes in Argentinian tango during the week as well as rock 'n' roll or salsa classes in the evening. Kitsch 1930s setting.

Opéra Bastille (**F** B3)
➔ *pl. de la Bastille (11ᵗʰ) Tel. 08 36 69 78 68 for information / reservations*
Opera, lyric opera, classical ballet. Reserve several weeks in advance.

SHOPPING

La Bague de Kenza (**F** C1)
➔ *106, rue Saint-Maur (11ᵗʰ) Tel. 01 43 14 93 15 Daily 9.30am–9pm.*
The best Algerian pastries in Paris. Wide choice of breads and savory specialties.

Cooperativa Cisternino (**F** C1)
➔ *108, rue Saint-Maur (11ᵗʰ) Tel. 01 48 01 05 02 Mon-Sat 10am–1.30pm, 4–8pm; Sun 10am–1.30pm.*
Reasonably priced

cheeses *(mozzarella pecorino, parmesan)* and quality *charcuterie* from the Iberian Peninsula.

Viaduc des Arts (**F** C4)
➔ *ave. Daumesnil (12ᵗʰ)*
Ceramics, tapestry, sculpture, cabinetmaking, painting and much more: over 45 designers and highly skilled craft-workers occupy the vaults of this viaduct, renovated in 1990.

Galerie Gaultier (**F** C3)
➔ *30, rue du Faubourg-Saint-Antoine (11ᵗʰ) Tel. 01 44 68 84 84 Mon-Sat 11am–7.30pm.*
Clothes and accessories by Jean-Paul, the *enfant terrible* of the French fashion world.

Bo Plastic (**F** C3)
➔ *31, rue de Charonne (11ᵗʰ) Tel. 01 53 36 73 16 Mon-Sat 11am–8pm.*
Plastic creations, mostly from the 60s and 70s, for collectors or 60s design junkies. Exhibitions too.

FNAC Bastille (**F** B3)
➔ *4, pl. de la Bastille (12ᵗʰ) Tel. 01 43 42 04 04 Mon-Sat 10am–8pm (until 10pm Wed and Fri).*
Unlike the other branches of FNAC, here music takes pride of place. Specialist service. Ticket booth for concerts.

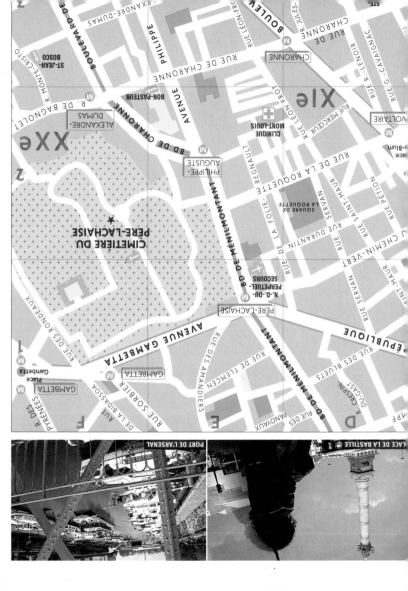

The map region:

BON-SECOURS
R. DU DAHOMEY
R. DE LA FORGE-ROYALE
R. ST-BERNARD
R. PAUL-E
HERBE
TITON
VOLTAIRE
RUE DES BOULETS
RUE DE MONTREUIL
AVRON
STE
NE

FAUBOURG SAINT-ANTOINE
RUE DU ★ FAUBOURG SAINT-ANTOINE
RUE DE MONTREUIL
STE-FAMILLE

HÔPITAL ST-ANTOINE
FAIDHERBE-CHALIGNY

XIIe

NATION (R.E.R.)
AVENUE TAILLEBOURG
Place de la Nation

RUE DE CÎTEAUX
RUE CROZATIER
CHALIGNY
RUE DE REUILLY
RUE C.-TILLIER
BOULEVARD DIDEROT
RUE DE PICPUS

BD DIDEROT
REUILLY-DIDEROT
SQ ST-CHARLES

4

0   150   300 m

D   E   E

MARCHÉ D'ALIGRE

PROMENADE PLANTÉE

---

orland bridge. The ginal Port de l'Arsenal, rmed in 1806 between e Seine and Canal St-artin, allowed the nsportation of wood craftworkers in the ubourg St-Antoine.

Faubourg aint-Antoine (**F** D4)
→ *rue du Faubourg-St-toine (11ᵗʰ/12ᵗʰ)*
▸m 1471, this *faubourg* thered around the abbey rowing community of rpenters, joiners, gilders d varnishers authorized work freely, outside of constraints of any poration. An urban mmunity slowly grew up

around the faubourg, where craftworkers remain. Several centuries of urbanization have shaped the lovely courtyard of l'Étoile-d'Or at n° 75 rue du Faubourg-St-Antoine. On the other side of the street, the Passage du Chantier reflects the continued craft-industry activity in the district. Next door, at n° 58, you can see the magnificent Bel-Air court-yard, now extremely over-grown, while at n° 74 there is the great courtyard of the Burgundians – its iron architecture influenced by the 19th-century industrial-ization of the area.

★ **Marché d'Aligre** (**F** C4)
→ *rue and place d'Aligre (12ᵗʰ) Tue–Sun 8am–1pm.*
From early morning the little Place d'Aligre is packed and you have to fight your way through the crowds to get to the fruit and vegetable stalls on Rue d'Aligre. On the square there are florists and stalls of bric-à-brac. In the Halle Beauvau, built in 1787, meat, dairy and *charcuterie* stallholders shout at the top of their voices touting for customers.
A delightful market, full of Mediterranean colors, and offering the lowest prices in the capital.

★ **Promenade Plantée or 'Coulée Verte'** (**F** C4)
→ *bd Diderot and ave. Daumesnil (12ᵗʰ)*
Laid out between 1988 and 1993, this walk stretches ¾ sq mile from the Bastille to the Bois de Vincennes. Passing over viaducts (including the Viaduct des Arts) and across foot-bridges, the pedestrian can see a succession of gardens, some elaborately planted, some left to grow wild. An astonishing walkway hangs suspended at window level. From the Jardin de Reuilly a cycle track takes you into the Bois de Vincennes.

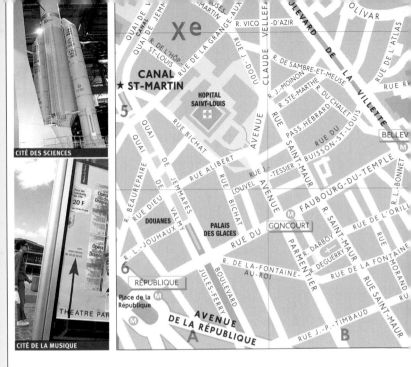

CITÉ DES SCIENCES

CITÉ DE LA MUSIQUE

THÉÂTRE PAR

On the map:
QUAI DE
CANAL
QUAI R. DE JEMP
ST-LOUIS
CANAL
★ ST-MARTIN
HOPITAL
SAINT-LOUIS
5
R. VICQ -D'AZIR
OLIVAR
BOULEVARD DE LA VILLETTE
RUE DE SAMBRE-ET-MEUSE
RUE DE L'ATLAS
RUE R
R.-MOINON
R. J.-DODU
CLAUDE
VELLEF
RUE J.-MOINON
R. STE-MARTHE
R. J. STE-MARTHE
RUE DU CHALET
PASS. HÉBRARD
RUE DU
SAINT-MAUR
BUISSON-ST-LOUIS
BELLEV
M
RUE BICHAT
QUAI DE
RUE ALIBERT
RUE J.-TESSIER
AVENUE
DE
JEMMAPES
RUE DIEU
R. BEAUREPAIRE
RUE BICHAT
LOUVEL
AVENUE
FAUBOURG-DU-TEMPLE
R. SAINT-MAUR
R. L.-BONNET
R. L.-JOUHAUX
VALMY
DOUANES
PALAIS
DES GLACES
RUE DU
M
GONCOURT
R. DARBOY
PARMENTIER
R. DEGUERRY
RUE DE L'ORILL
RUE
R.-DE-LA-FONTAINE-
AU-ROI
RUE DE LA FONTAINE
RUE
MORAND
RÉPUBLIQUE
Place de la
République
M
JULES-FERRY
BOULEVARD
AVENUE
DE LA RÉPUBLIQUE
A
RUE SAINT-MAUR
RUE J.-P.-TIMBAUD
B
6
Xe

★ Canal St-Martin (G A5)
Carved out between 1822
and 1825, at the request of
Napoleon I, to provide the
people of Paris with
drinking water, this canal
has become one of Paris'
most romantic spots. Its
planted banks and series
of locks, the metal foot
bridges and little gardens
that spread over 3 miles
are reminiscent of a Paris
that has now disappeared.
The legendary Hôtel du
Nord (immortalized in 1938
by Marcel Carné), was at
one time threatened with
destruction, but survived
and in 1996 was converted
into a restaurant.

**★ Parc de La Villette /
Canal de l'Ourcq (G** D1)
→ 221, ave. Jean-Jaurès (11th)
One of the most amazing
landscaped gardens in
Paris, completed in 1991,
on the site of the former
halles (covered market) of
La Villette. A decidedly
urban park, designed as a
'town garden' with main
thoroughfares, square,
walks and gardens. The
meadows of the Cercle
and the Triangle have a
total of 17 acres of grass.
The blue path of the
cinema promenade snakes
its way over nearly two
miles, crossing 10 themed
gardens. The park's lawns

come to life each summer
with concerts, displays and
a free open-air film festival
attracting huge audiences
from the city, longing to
be outdoors. A cycle track
offers a pleasant ride along
the Canal de l'Ourcq all the
way to Meaux, tens of
miles away.
**★ Cité des Sciences
et de l'Industrie (G** D1)
→ 30, ave. Corentin-Cariou
(19th) Tel. 01 40 05 80 00
Since 1986 this has
occupied the buildings of
the former slaughterhouses
and animal markets of La
Villette. The permanent
exhibition 'Explora'
consists of several displays

(space, the environment,
the ocean, etc) organized
around one central area.
For children there are
participatory exhibits and
games, encouraging them
to literally come to grips
with scientific and techni-
information, whilst 'Techn
Cité' focuses on the vario
different phases of an
industrial project. The
Géode building has an
hemispheric cinema scree
1,196 sq yards in size.
**★ Cité / Musée de
la Musique (G** D2)
→ Parc de la Villette
221, ave. Jean-Jaurès (19th,
Tel. 01 44 84 45 45
This site is dedicated

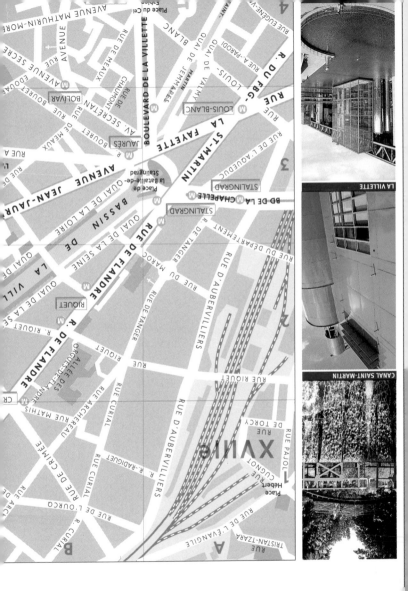

Place du Cel...
Éphéb...

AVENUE MATHURIN-MORE...
RUE EUGÈNE-V...

AVENUE MATHURIN-MORE...
AVENUE
RUE DE MEAUX
RUE DE SECRÉ...
AVENUE SECRÉ...
ÉDOUAR...

QUAI DE VALMY
QUAI DE JEMMAPES
QUAI DE JEMMAPES
RUE A.-PARODI-V...
R. DU FBG-
RUE DU FBG-
LOUIS-

BOULEVARD DE LA VILLETTE

RUE DE MEAUX
RUE DE CHAUMONT
AV. SECRÉTAN
RUE BOURET
RUE BOURET
BOLIVAR Ⓜ
JAURÈS Ⓜ

RUE
LOUIS-BLANC Ⓜ
LA VILLETTE Ⓜ

FAYETTE
ST-MARTIN
AVENUE JEAN-JAUR...

RUE DE L'AQUEDUC
RUE A...
RUE DE...
L'...

BASSIN DE LA LOIRE
QUAI DE LA LOIRE

Place de la Bataille-de-QUAI DE LA LOIRE
Stalingrad

STALINGRAD Ⓜ
STALINGRAD Ⓜ
BD DE LA CHAPELLE Ⓜ

RUE DE FLANDRE
RUE DE LA SEINE
QUAI DE LA SE...
QUAI DE LA SE...
QUAI DE
LA VILL...

RIQUET Ⓜ

R. DU DÉPARTEMENT
R. DE TANGER
R. DE TANGER
RUE DE TANGER
RUE DU MAROC

RUE D'AUBERVILLIERS

R. DE RIQUET
R. DE FLANDRE

RUE RIQUET
RUE RIQUET
ALLÉE DES
ORGUES-DE-FLANDRE

RUE MATHIS
RUE ARCHEREAU
RUE CURIAL
RUE ARCHEREAU

RUE D'AUBERVILLIERS

RUE RIQUET

XVIIIe

R.-RADIQUET
RUE CURIAL
RUE CURIAL
RUE DE CRIMÉE
RUE DE CRIMÉE
RUE DE...

RUE DE L'OURCQ
R. CURIAL
BD...
RUE TRISTAN-TZARA
RUE DE L'ÉVANGILE

Place
Hébert
RUE
CUGNOT

RUE
DE TORCY
RUE PAJOL
CR...
CR

LA VILLETTE

CANAL SAINT-MARTIN

Along the canals, Paris past and Paris present stand side by side. A walk along the banks of the Canal St-Martin is full of old-fashioned charm. The Canal de l'Ourq, by contrast, continues as far as La Villette, where a thoroughly 21st-century park suddenly appears out of nowhere. Further south the Park des Buttes-Chaumont, reformed in 1864 to rehabilitate the surrounding slum area, has given birth to a respectable residential district. Below it are the working-class villages of Belleville and Ménilmontant, rich with the influence of immigrants from Asia and the Orient.

LE BARATIN

RESTAURANTS

Benesti (**G** C6)
→ 108, bd de Belleville (20ᵗʰ) Tel. 01 44 55 44 55 Tue-Sun.
Wonderful Jewish Tunisian snacks: falafel sandwiches, brik, choudchouka, Tunisian salads, mint tea and pastries. A place where people eat lots and talk even more! An extra-ordinary taste of the Mediterranean.
Dinner 50–70F.

Le Baratin (**G** C5)
→ 3, rue Jouye-Rouve (20ᵗʰ) Tel. 01 43 49 39 70 Tue-Sat noon–2.30pm, 8.30–11.30pm.
Impressive wine list compiled by patron Olivier Camus (there are 200 different wines on the menu). Excellent cuisine based around seasonal availability. Friendly atmosphere, unpretentious setting.
Lunch menu 73F.

La Boulangerie (**G** D6)
→ 15, rue des Panoyaux (20ᵗʰ) Tel. 01 43 58 45 45 Daily except Sat lunch.
This restaurant at the front of a traditional bakery, opened its doors in May 1999. The décor is as delicious as the cooking: effilochade of

dried duck with cardamom and creamed lentils, salt beef followed by Ménilmontant tart for dessert. Set menu, lunch 68F, dinner 98F.

L'Heure Bleue (**G** D4)
→ 57, rue Arthur Rozier (19ᵗʰ) Tel. 01 42 39 18 07 Mon-Fri noon–2.30pm, 7–10.45pm;
Sat eve only 7–10.45pm
Good traditional cuisine with a south west touch (duck confit, foie gras) but also a wide range of very good vegetarian dishes (vegetable ravioli, savoury tarts). Set menu 65F (lunchtime only); à la carte 120-150F.

L'Atlantide (**G** C3)
→ 7, ave. Laumière (19ᵗʰ) Tel. 01 42 45 09 81 Tue-Sun 7.30pm–midnight.
Dine here and sample the best Berber specialties: couscous of fine semolina served with a choice of sauce or fresh steamed vegetables. The meat is succulent, particularly the tajine dishes (with dried fruits or vegetables). À la carte 150F.

La Cave Gourmande (**G** D4)
→ 10, rue du Gᵃˡ-Brunet (19ᵗʰ) Tel. 01 40 40 03 30 Mon-Fri noon–2pm, 7–10pm.
Restaurant, delicatessen

U PASCALOU · MARCHÉ DE BELLEVILLE · ÉPICERIE LE CAIRE

and wine merchant where fine food is always on offer. The choice is somewhat limited, but the menu changes daily. Set menu only, 170F.

Krung Thep (G C5)
→ 93, rue Julien-Lacroix (20th) Tel. 01 43 66 83 74 Daily 6pm–midnight.
It's difficult to imagine that behind these smoked-glass windows lurks one of the the best Thai restaurants in Paris. Exotic setting, efficient service and, above all, delicious food with subtle and unusual combinations of flavors: sweet salad with banana flower, wrapped chicken, *pat thaï* (noodles sautéed with shrimp)... If the place is full, go straight to Lao Siam, 49, rue de Belleville, instead.

CAFÉS, BARS, MUSIC VENUES

La Maroquinerie (G D6)
→ 23, rue Boyer (20th) Tel. 01 40 33 30 60 Closed Sun.
This fashionable venue, with its ultra-modern décor used to be an old leather workshop, tucked away in a courtyard. Its concerts, exhibitions readings and debates

encourage meetings between local inhabitants and artists.
Daily specials 50–60F.
Lou Pascalou (G D6)
→ 14, rue des Panoyaux (20th) Tel. 01 46 36 78 10 Daily 9am–2pm.
Understated, but cozy, a limited number of tables and a terrace, obliging waiters... A popular, no-nonsense place, like its regulars. Rock or world music concerts and, occasionally, theater evenings.
Le Soleil (G C6)
→ 136, bd de Ménilmontant (20th). Tel. 01 46 36 47 44 Daily until 2am.
Four rows of tables on the terrace spill out onto the sidewalk, tempting passersby. Sip a mint tea, a *pastis*, or a draught beer. Attracts a friendly, mixed crowd.
Aux Folies (G C5)
→ 8, rue de Belleville (19th) Tel. 01 46 36 65 98 Daily 6am–midnight.
The neon sign conjures up the old Belleville. Here, in the 1930s, a café-theater drew the biggest names, from Édith Piaf to Yves Montand. Amar, who has now taken over the venue, has kept the original

décor. An unpretentious place where you can have a drink at the bar, or on the terrace, and sit watching the world go by.
Cité de la Musique (G D2)
→ Parc de la Villette 221, ave. Jean-Jaurès (19th) Tel. 01 44 84 45 00 Concerts 90–200F. www.cite-musique.fr
An oval-shaped auditorium seating 800-1,200. Weekend concerts tend to be organized around a particular theme. Jazz classical, contemporary and traditional music concerts. There is also a multi-media library and information center on music and dance (Tue-Sun until 6pm).
Le Trabendo (G D2)
→ 211, ave Jean-Jaurès (20th) Tel. 01 42 54 07 47 for program information.
Formerly known as Hot Brass, this auditorium seats 700 and is filled with the graffiti art of Futura 2000. Modern venue for rock, world music and jazz concerts. Entrance 80–120F.

SHOPPING

Marché de Belleville (G B5-C6)

→ M° Belleville and Ménilmontant
Every Tuesday and Friday the central divider strip of the Boulevard de Belleville plays host to one of the largest markets in Paris. Hundreds of colorful stalls selling fruit, vegetables, spices ... the crowds are extraordinary.
Épicerie Le Caire (G C5)
→ 63, rue de Belleville (19th) Tel. 01 42 06 06 01 Tue–Sun 10am–10pm.
Adel Moussa's grocery store resembles a *souk*: olives, spices, cheese, rice, semolina and Egyptian specialties (cardamom-flavored coffee, *mammoul* with dates, pistachio or walnuts *borek* with cheese or spinach ...).
Nani (G D5)
→ 104, rue de Belleville (20th) Tel. 01 47 97 38 05 Sun–Fri 8am–7.30pm.
Since 1962 Nani has made the locals salivate. The store's narrow front hides a small, long pâtisserie. On the left are classics like lemon tarts, strawberry gâteaux, *millefeuille* pastries... on the right, a mountain of oriental pastries: *makroud*, *baklava*, *oreillettes* with honey...).

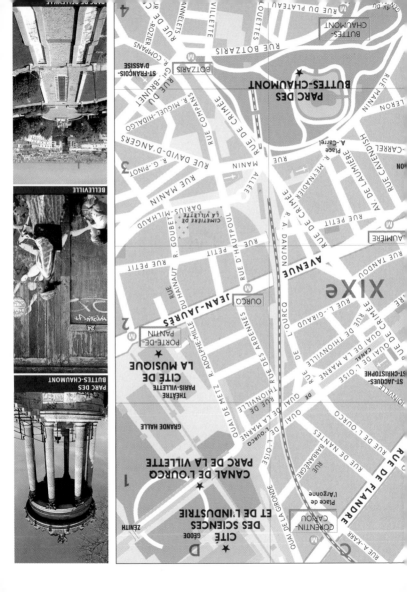

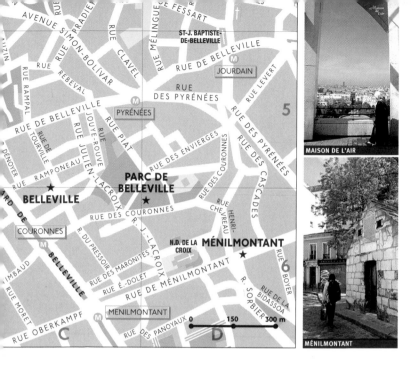

music in all forms.
tuated to the south
the Parc de La Villette,
houses the exclusive
nservatoire and
concert hall which stages
ncerts throughout the
ar. The museum, opened
1997, acquires, restores
d exhibits a collection
what is now more than
500 instruments dating
m the Renaissance to
e present day.

**Parc des Buttes-
aumont (G** C4)
Rues Manin and Botzaris
th) Daily 7.30am–11pm
om in winter).
iginally part of Napoleon
s desire to make Paris a

healthier place to live in,
this park was renovated
in 1864 taking over slum
areas and giving the
northeast of the capital its
own large area of greenery.
The architect Davioud
transformed the former
quarries, carving them
into a lake and creating
a series of waterfalls,
streams, embankments
and plantations. It is a
stunning park where the
paths plunge into the
undergrowth, clamber up
rocks and then, suddenly,
open up onto higher land.

★ **Belleville (G** C6)
→ Between rue and bd de
Belleville (19th / 20th)

Even at dawn the Boulevard
de Belleville is busy, with
lively discussions and card
games going on. The café-
terraces are packed with
people and from the
surrounding stalls, the air
is filled with the delicious
smell of mint tea and the
sound of oriental music.
Rue de Belleville, which
runs to the top of the hill, is
a regular little Chinatown,
while grocers, restaurants,
cafés and bazaars run the
length of the Rue des
Pyrénées.

★ **Parc de Belleville (G** D6)
→ Rue des Couronnes, rue
Piat and rue Jouye-Rouve (20th)
Rue Piat, which in the 19th

century lead the way to
two windmills, now
emerges in a lovely park
built on the buttresses of
a former gypsum quarry.
Spectacular views of the
capital. Workshops and
exhibitions at the Maison
de l'Air (at the top of the
park).

★ **Ménilmontant (G** D6)
→ Rue de Ménilmontant (20th)
These streets have not
entirely lost their appeal:
Rue des Cascades has
charming houses and Rue
de la Mare has a pretty
bridge over the railway
track. Rue des Envierges
takes you right back to the
Parc de Belleville.

CHAPELLE SAINT-LOUIS

MANUFACTURE DES GOBELINS

★ **Institut du Monde Arabe** (H B1)
→ *1, rue des Fossés-St-Bernard (5th)*
Tel. 01 40 51 38 38
Daily 10am–6pm.
This amazing building designed by Jean Nouvel is an adaptation of an Arab-Hispanic architectural concept using contemporary materials. The museum is dedicated to the art and culture of Arab and Islamic civilizations, as is the library, specialist book-store and also the cinema, concerts, dance performances and temporary exhibitions.

★ **Arènes de Lutèce** (H A1)
→ *49, rue Monge (5th) Daily.*
Discovered in 1869 while clearing the Rue Monge, these remains of a Gallo-Roman amphitheater were later incorporated into a peaceful garden which has today become a sports field – a firm favorite with children and locals who like playing *boules*.

★ **Muséum National d'Histoire Naturelle** (H B2)
→ *57, rue Cuvier (5th)*
Tel. 01 40 79 30 00
Mon, Wed-Sun 10am–6pm (Thu until 10pm).
The Paleontology and

Anatomy galleries of the Natural History Museum both resemble an 18th-century surgery, full of strange curiosities. They are also intact: waxed parquet floors, original windows and old, hand-written labels, providing fodder for a formidable tour of the human body and a fascinating journey through the world of fossils, dinosaur bones, giant birds and insects. In the Evolution gallery is a permanent exhibition on the evolution of life. The immense collection of stuffed animals on show in the nave is frighteningly

lifelike and impressive in size.

★ **Jardin des Plantes** (H B2)
→ *Rue Cuvier, rue Buffon and place Valhubert (5th)*
Tel. 01 40 79 30 00
Daily 10am–5pm.
Facing the Grande Galerie the botanical garden and flower beds; on the right are two large glasshouses (Mexican and Tropical). The large maze takes you past rare species of plants, whe the cries of various exotic animals can be heard from the zoo. In 1635, the royal garden of medicinal plants became the first park in Paris to open its gates to

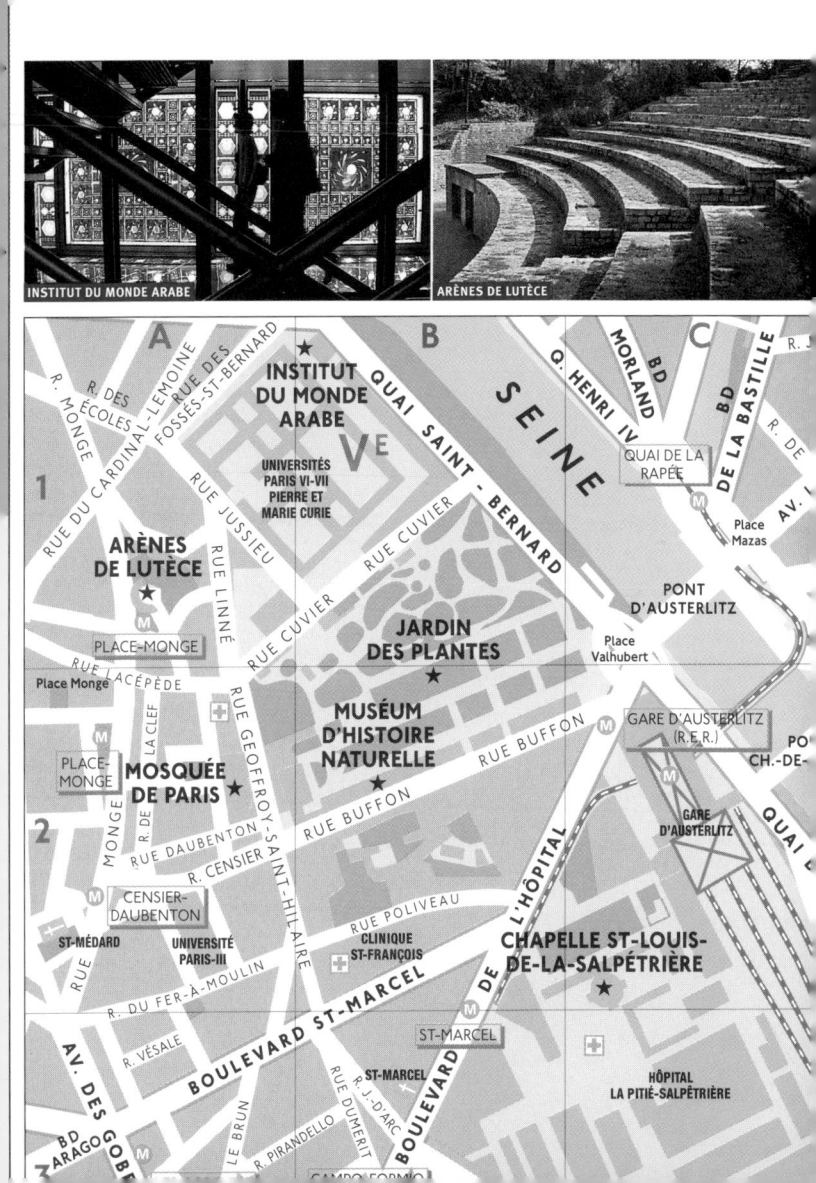

INSTITUT DU MONDE ARABE

ARÈNES DE LUTÈCE

The immense Bibliothèque Nationale (1997) is seen as a symbol for the east side of Paris, an area which has totally changed over the past two decades. The industrial waste-lands of Bercy and Austerlitz have provided architects and town planners with invaluable experimental freedom, resulting in the Institut du Monde Arabe in 1987, the Ministère des Finances in 1989, the Parc de Bercy in 1994 and various new residential districts. Below the Jardin des Plantes the boulevards lead to the Place d'Italie and, toward the Porte de Choisy, to the towers of Chinatown (1970), erected at the foot of the Butte-aux-Cailles.

ZIRYAB   LE TRAIN BLEU

RESTAURANTS

Le Temps des Cerises (H A4)
→ 18, rue de la Butte-aux-Cailles (13th)
Tel. 01 45 89 69 48
Mon-Sat noon–2pm, 7.30–11.45pm.
Workers' cooperative offering an informal place to eat. Home-cooking with the occasional exotic influence. Generous portions, set 3-course menu at 78F. If it's full, try the nearby *Chez Gladines* (Basque specialties) or *Chez Paul* (a little more expensive).

Phô Ban Cuon 14 (H B4)
→ 129, ave. de Choisy (13th)
Tel. 01 45 83 61 15
Daily 9am–11pm.
On the borders of Chinatown, this is the hangout for *phô* enthusiasts (it is available all day). The Vietnamese noodle soup served here is amongst the best in Paris. Around 70F.

Le Ziryab (H B1)
→ Institut du Monde Arabe 1, rue des Fossés-St-Bernard (5th). Tel. 01 53 10 10 17
Tue-Sun
noon–3pm (restaurant),
3.30-6pm (tearoom).
At the top of the Institut du Monde Arabe, there is a bird's-eye view of Notre Dame, north to the Bastille and beyond: a magnificent setting in which to savour a quail *pastilla* (110F), a lamb tajine (140F) or maybe just a mint tea made with fresh leaves (20F).

Le Petit Marguery (H A3)
→ 9, bd de Port-Royal (13th)
Tel. 01 43 31 58 59 Tue-Sat
noon–2pm, 7.30–10.15pm.
The epitome of the French bistro, run by the adorable Cousin brothers. Bourgeois cuisine and game in season. Generous portions and regional wine. Tradition at its best. Set menu 165F.

Etchegorry (H A4)
→ 41–43, rue Croulebarbe (13th) Tel. 01 44 08 83 51
Mon-Sat noon–2.30pm, 7–10.30pm.
South-west French cuisine, especially influenced by the Basque country. Reasonable prices. Set menu 145F, gastronomic menu (with *foie gras*) 180F.

Le Train Bleu (H D1)
→ Gare de Lyon
20, bd Diderot (12th)
Tel. 01 43 43 09 06
Daily 11.30am–3pm, 7–11pm
One of a kind: a station restaurant in a listed historic building. Extraordinary décor with

A FOLIE EN TÊTE   BERCY VILLAGE   LES ABEILLES

frescos depicting the stops along the Paris-Lyon-Méditerranée (PLM) line, statues, moldings and 1900s furniture. Eager service and good classic cuisine: creamed lentils with bacon and browned croûtons, pike dumplings with crawfish. Set menu 255F.

CAFÉS, TEAROOMS

Bercy Village (H F4)
→ Cour St-Émilion (12th)
These former Bercy *chais* (wine cellars) are the perfect place to stop for a drink as they have now been refurbished and turned into café-restaurants.

Salon de Thé de la Mosquée de Paris (H A2)
→ 39, rue Geoffroy-St-Hilaire (5th)
Tel. 01 43 31 18 14 Daily 8am–11.30pm (tearoom)
Tel. 01 43 31 18 14 (baths)
Women: Mon, Wed-Sat 10am–9pm (Fri 2–9pm)
Men: Tue 2–9pm;
Sun 10am–9pm.
Small tables under the olive and fig trees, the murmur of the fountain, the sweet smell of incense: this setting is straight out of *The Arabian Nights*. Moorish interior and sofas inside

the mosque. Eat a full meal or simply sample the crunchy honey-, almond-, or orange flower-flavored pastries. But before that, why not indulge yourself in the hammam's tempting steam rooms?

BARS, CINEMA, MUSIC VENUES

La Folie en tête (H A4)
→ 33, rue de la Butte-aux-Cailles (13th)
Tel. 01 45 80 65 99
Mon–Sat 5pm–2am.
A lively little café decorated with wooden musical instruments from all over the world, in the heart of the old village of Butte-aux-Cailles. Contemporary art exhibitions, occasional concerts, storytelling and theater.

Batofar (H E3)
→ Port de la Gare, opposite 11, quai Mauriac (13th) Tel. 01 56 29 10 00 (times vary depending on the program).
The latest addition to the trendy fleet of restaurants anchored at the foot of the Bibliothèque Nationale. Steel hull and interior: urban films and exhibitions, electronic music and international

DJs – and a crowd on hand to rock the boat!
Guinguette Pirate (H E3)
→ Port de la Gare, facing n° 11, quai Mauriac (13th) Tel. 01 56 29 10 20
Daily from 7pm.
Eclectic clientele and a charged atmosphere in this wooden junk built in Saigon in 1970. Its neighbor, the barge *Makara*, has a different program of music every evening: rock, world music, dub, jazz, reggae, funk, trip hop. Shows for children.

Gaumont Grand Écran Italie (H A4)
→ 30, pl. d'Italie (13th)
Tel. 01 45 80 86 78
Spectacular films shown on the biggest screen in Paris (860 sq ft). Housed in a monochrome, aluminium building designed by Kenzo Tange.

SHOPPING

Galeries d'Art de la rue Louise-Weiss (H C3-C4)
These art galleries now occupy the workshops which once flourished in this former industrial district. They continue the tradition of the great 'Frigos', the former refrigerated warehouses

of Bercy converted into studios which have, since 1980, welcomed into their thousands of square feet at n° 91, quai Panhard-et-Levassor, a plethora of painters, sculptors, architects and musicians.
Les Abeilles (H A4)
→ 21, rue de la Butte-aux-Cailles (13th)
Tel. 01 45 81 43 48
Tue-Sat 11am–7pm.
Fifty types of honey from all over France.
Mavrommatis (H A2)
→ 47, rue Censier (5th)
Tel. 01 45 35 96 50
Daily 9am–10pm.
A lovely top-of-the-range Greek deli selling various *meze*: talassini, stuffed vine leaves, aubergine or pepper *caviar* (puréed with a garlic and olive oil marinade). Wide choice of Greek and Cypriot wines.
Marché de la Place Monge (H A2)
→ Wed, Fri and Sun.
Attractive little food market close to the Rue Mouffetard.
Tang Frères (H B2)
→ 48, ave. d'Ivry (13th)
Tel. 01 45 70 80 00
Tue-Sun 9am–7.30pm.
The largest and most famous Asian super-market in the capital, a few steps from Place d'Italie (off the map).

JARDIN DES PLANTES MUSÉUM D'HISTOIRE NATURELLE MOSQUÉE DE PARIS

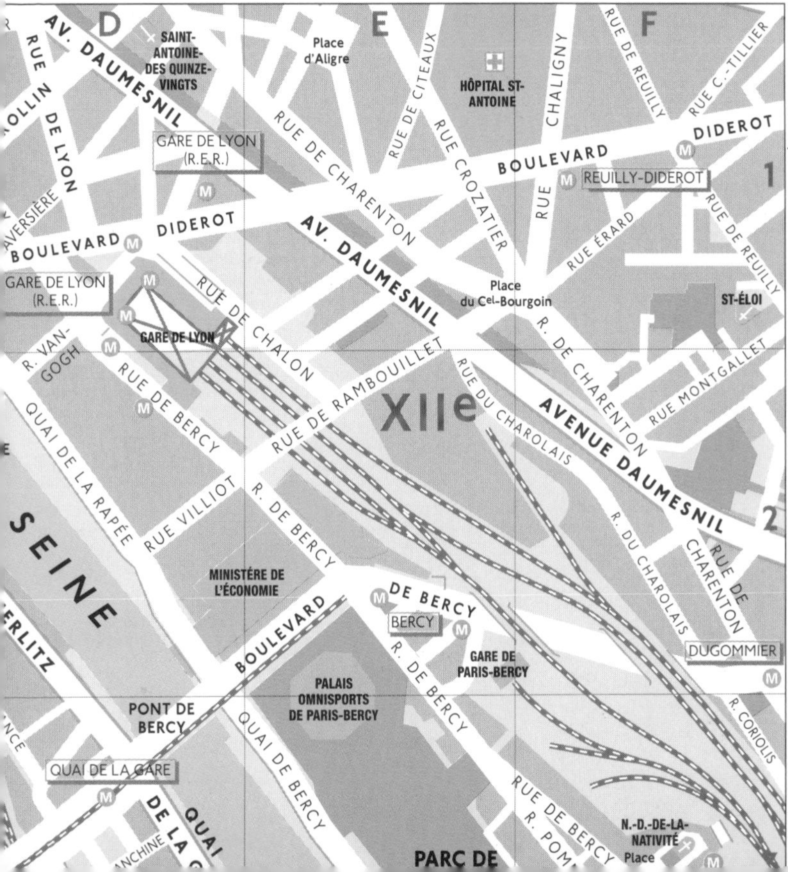

D · E · F

SAINT-ANTOINE-DES-QUINZE-VINGTS

Place d'Aligre

HÔPITAL ST-ANTOINE

AV. DAUMESNIL

RUE ROLLIN

RUE DE LYON

RUE DE CITEAUX

RUE DE CHARENTON

RUE CROZATIER

RUE CHALIGNY

RUE DE REUILLY

RUE C.-TILLIER

DIDEROT

GARE DE LYON (R.E.R.)

DIDEROT

BOULEVARD

REUILLY-DIDEROT

1

TRAVERSIÈRE

BOULEVARD

DIDEROT

AV. DAUMESNIL

RUE ÉRARD

RUE DE REUILLY

GARE DE LYON (R.E.R.)

RUE DE CHALON

Place du Cel-Bourgoin

ST-ÉLOI

R. VAN-GOGH

GARE DE LYON

RUE DE BERCY

RUE DE RAMBOUILLET

RUE DU CHAROLAIS

AVENUE DAUMESNIL

RUE DE CHARENTON

RUE MONTGALLET

XIIe

2

SEINE

QUAI DE LA RAPÉE

RUE VILLIOT

R. DE BERCY

R. DU CHAROLAIS

RUE DE CHARENTON

AUSTERLITZ

MINISTÈRE DE L'ÉCONOMIE

BOULEVARD

DE BERCY

BERCY

GARE DE PARIS-BERCY

DUGOMMIER

FRANCE

PONT DE BERCY

R. DE BERCY

PALAIS OMNISPORTS DE PARIS-BERCY

R. CORIOLIS

QUAI DE LA GARE

QUAI DE BERCY

TOLBIAC

QUAI DE LA GARE

RUE DE BERCY

R. POM-

N.-D.-DE-LA-NATIVITÉ Place

PARC DE

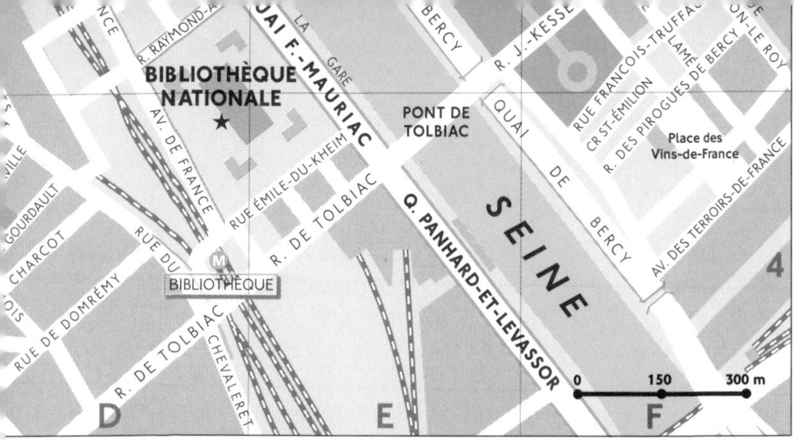
BIBLIOTHÈQUE
NATIONALE
PONT DE
TOLBIAC
SEINE
Place des
Vins-de-France
R. RAYMOND-A
LA
GARE
BERCY
R. J.-KESSEL
RUE FRANÇOIS-TRUFFAUT
CR ST-ÉMILION
R. DES PIROGUES DE BERCY
AV. DE FRANCE
RUE ÉMILE-DU-KHEIM
R. DE TOLBIAC
Q. PANHARD-ET-LEVASSOR
QUAI
DE
BERCY
AV. DES TERROIRS-DE-FRANCE
GOURDAULT
CHARCOT
RUE DU
CHEVALERET
RUE DE DOMRÉMY
R. DE TOLBIAC
BIBLIOTHÈQUE
0
150
300 m
D
E
F
4

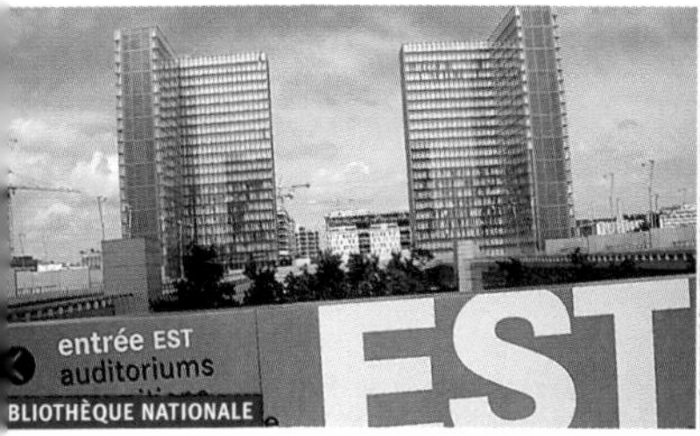
entrée EST
auditoriums
EST
BLIOTHÈQUE NATIONALE

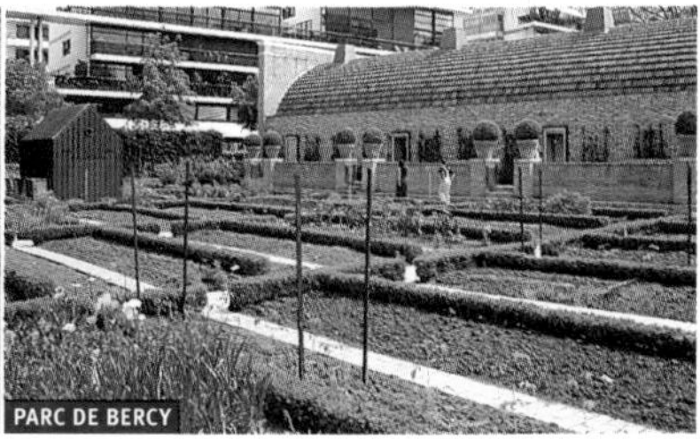
PARC DE BERCY

e public. It was taken
er by the Natural History
useum in 1793.

Mosquée de Paris (**H** A2)
1, pl. du Puits-de-l'Ermite
h) Tel. 01 43 31 18 14
osed Fri.
is temple to the Muslim
igion was the first to be
ilt in Paris (1922-6). It
s a rich Mediterranean
luence and is a feast
the eyes: mosaics,
darwood carvings and
e finest lattice work –
ich interior created by
cal craftsmen. The fairy-
e mosque is arranged
ound a courtyard and
door gardens and has a
mmam, a *salon de thé*, restaurant and stores at n°s 39-41, rue Geoffroy-St-Hilaire.

★ **Chapelle St-Louis-de-la-Salpêtrière** (**H** C2)
→ *47, bd de l'Hôpital (13th)*
Daily 8.30am–6.30pm.
Located within the walls of one of Paris' oldest hospitals and built at the request of Louis XIV, this chapel (1677) is in the form of a Greek cross topped with an astonishing octogonal dome. It now provides a setting for concerts and exhibitions.

★ **Manufacture des Gobelins** (**H** A3)
→ *42, rue des Gobelins (5th)*
Tel. 01 44 08 52 00
Tue-Thu at 2pm and 2.45pm
This royal tapestry workshop, founded in 1601 by Henry IV, was appointed furniture-maker to the Crown in 1667. It also contains 17th- and 18th-century tapestries designed by Van der Meulen and beautiful religious gold artefacts.

★ **Bibliothèque Nationale de France** (**H** D4)
→ *quai François-Mauriac (13th) Tel. 01 53 79 59 59*
Tue-Sat 10am–8pm; Sun noon–7pm (reception, east visitors hall). www.bnf.fr
The four book-shaped towers of the 'Très Grande Bibliothèque' were devised by Dominique Perrault. They hold some 10 million works which cover more than 260 miles of shelving. There are advanced reference systems and the latest in conservation techniques. The reading rooms are arranged around a delightful indoor garden. Temporary exhibitions.

★ **Parc de Bercy** (**H** E3)
→ *quai de Bercy (12th) Daily.*
In 1994 the wine storehouses of Bercy gave way to the development of a 33-acre park: botanical gardens, lawns, an orchard, a kitchen garden and a romantic-style garden.

RAINS & STATIONS

x stations serve the ain regions of France: are du Nord (north), are de l'Est (northeast), are de Lyon (southeast), are d'Austerlitz outhwest), Gare ontparnasse (west, uthwest), Gare Saint-zare (northwest).

GV: Links Paris to veral major cities antes, Lyon) in France d the rest of Europe.

halys: Paris–nsterdam (4¼ hours), a Brussels (1½ hours).

urostar: Paris–London hours).

NCF information
Tel. 08 36 35 35 35 35

TAXIS

The white sign 'Taxi' indicates that taxis are free. When they are in use they display a small orange light.
Taxis Bleus
→ Tel. 01 49 36 10 10
Taxis G7
→ Tel. 01 47 39 47 39

CARS

Documentation
You may be required to show your insurance, vehicle registration documents and your driving license.
Speed limits
50 kmph (30 mph) in town.
Parking
(10F per hour) Mon-Fri, and Sat depending on the area. Purchase tickets from parking ticket machines, using the correct change. Free parking on Sun and public holidays and in some areas on Sat and during August.
Car pounds
Badly parked cars will be towed away to a car pound. To retrieve your vehicle, contact the nearest police station or the police headquarters:
→ Tel. 01 53 71 53 53

---

frescos in the dining m and an outrageous rror which has pride of ce at reception. gle rooms start at 325F. uble rooms are light and acious with 2 large beds, F.

tel Gilden Magenta F1)

35, rue Yves-Toudic (10th)
01 42 40 17 72

s establishment, tucked ay in a quiet little road tween République and Canal Saint-Martin, ers well-equipped rooms m 380F. Pleasant patio ere you can eat break-st; there is also the option using the kitchen. ductions for groups of ung people (by advance servation).

)0–500F

tel du Globe (A C2)
15, rue des Quatre-Vents
h) Tel. 01 43 26 35 50

Closed Aug.
Gorgeous 17th-century building. The interior decoration is eccentric but appealing. The rooms have floral drapes, exposed beams and stonework, stylish furniture and fresh flowers. From 410F.
Hôtel Esméralda (A D2)
→ 4, rue St-Julien-le-Pauvre (5th) Tel. 01 43 54 19 20
In a cobbled street, this 17th-century building giving onto the Square Vivienne houses a 19-room institution. Quirky little hotel with a garden, a view of Notre Dame, exposed stone walls, red velvet sofas, plants, uneven floors and a cat! Book well in advance. From 450–520F.
Hôtel de l'Espérance (A E4)
→ 5, rue Pascal (5th)
Tel. 01 47 07 10 99
Hotel situated at the bottom of Rue Mouffetard, with 38 lovely rooms, each

different to the next: pastel tones, floral curtains, four-poster beds. Breakfast is served in the small garden in good weather. From 440–550F.
Familia Hôtel (A E2)
→ 11, rue des Écoles (5th)
Tel. 01 43 54 55 27
The patron is very helpful to guests. Exposed beams or stonework, balconies with flowers, old-fashioned furniture and carpets, frescos of Paris, and a view of Notre Dame. From 460F. Just next door, the brand new Hôtel Minerve, owned by the same proprietor, offers the same service.
Hôtel des Croisés (E B5)
→ 63, rue Saint-Lazare (9th)
Tel. 01 48 74 78 24
Superb retro-style reception (wrought-iron elevator, red carpets) and period-style rooms from 470F. Double rooms (500F) are very spacious, fitted out with Art-Deco style

---

Roissy
Charles-
de-Gaulle
30 km

PARIS

15 km

Orly

N ↑

AIRPORTS

Flight information
→ Tel. 08 36 68 15 15
→ www. adp.fr
General information
Roissy Charles-
de-Gaulle (CDG)
→ Tel. 01 48 62 22 80
Orly
→ Tel. 01 49 75 52 52

PARIS AIRPORTS LINKS

Paris to Roissy CDG
RER B
→ Direct to CDG2 and
courtesy bus to CDG 1.
Roissybus
→ Rue Scribe, M° Opéra
Price 48F.
Air France shuttle
→ Porte Maillot, Étoile,
Montparnasse. Price 60F.
Paris to Orly
Orlyval
→ RER B to Antony, then
Orlyval. Price 57F.
Orlybus
→ In front of RER Denfert-
Rochereau. Price 35F.
Air France shuttle
→ M° Montparnasse
Invalides. Price 45F.

Arrivées

Aérogare 2 Terminal 2

AIRPORT

Except otherwise stated, the prices given are for a double room with en-suite bathroom. In peak season, make reservations at least a month in advance.

YOUTH HOSTELS

Price per person. Single or double rooms and accommodation in dormitories.

Résidence Bastille (F C3)
→ 151, ave. Ledru-Rollin, (11th) Tel. 01 43 79 53 86
Modern building with 150 beds. From 125–175F for a single room (including breakfast).

Hotels M. I. J. E. (C E4)
→ 6, rue de Fourcy (4th) Tel. 01 42 74 23 45
Right in the middle of the Marais, two 17th-century buildings and a medieval house have been converted into this youth hostel. Exceptional setting, comfortable and

relaxed atmosphere. 160F for the dormitories (reserved for 18–30 year-olds), 185F for a double room, breakfast included. Set dinner for 60F.

UNDER 250F

Hôtel Vicq d'Azir (G A4)
→ 21, rue Vicq d'Azir (10th) Tel. 01 42 08 06 70
Close to the Canal Saint-Martin, 70 very modest rooms, some with a view over a verdant little courtyard. From 117F (197F with shower).

Hôtel Henri-IV (A D1)
→ 25, pl. Dauphine (1st) Tel. 01 43 54 44 53
Fabulous location on the very chic Place Dauphine. True, this 16th-century hotel is rather spartan, if not run down, but the rooms have views onto the prettiest square in Paris. From 215F (280F with shower). Book in advance.

Hôtel du Palais (C C3)
→ 2, quai de la Mégisserie (1st) Tel. 01 42 36 98 25
Currently undergoing restoration work. The rooms which have already been renovated are much brighter and offer a view over the Île de la Cité. Ask for a room with double glazing. From 36F (shower and WC on the same floor).

250–400F

Hôtel Sainte-Marie (C C1)
→ 6, rue de la Ville-Neuve (2nd) Tel. 01 42 33 21 61
Close to the Grands Boulevards. Attractive, quiet rooms from 250F (340F with bathroom). Friendly reception.

Hôtel du Séjour (C D2)
→ 36, rue du Grenier-Saint-Lazare (3rd) Tel. 01 48 87 40 36
Near the Pompidou center

in the Halles area, this hotel offers modest, but recently redecorated rooms. Small interior courtyard. From 280F.

Hôtel Eiffel Rive Gauche (E C4)
→ 6, rue du Gros-Caillou (7th) Tel. 01 45 51 24 56
Four floors built around a small patio. The somewhat scruffy rooms are gradually being done up in a Provençal style. Two small double rooms (305F no shower) have a view of the Eiffel tower; from 445F with shower.

Hôtel Jeanne d'Arc (C E3)
→ 3, rue de Jarente (4th) Tel. 01 48 87 62 11
This 17th-century hotel is on the corner of a quiet, pretty street in the Marais. It has been decorated with the works of artists who are regulars to the hotel... they may not be to everybody's taste. There

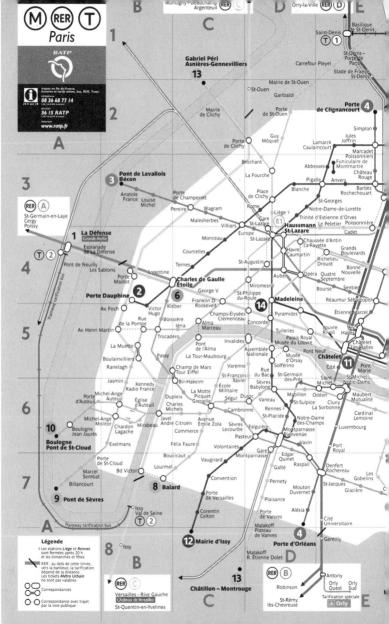